A Guide to the Common Core Writing Workshop

Middle School Grades

Lucy Calkins

HEINEMANN ◆ PORTSMOUTH, NH

Heinemann
361 Hanover Street
Portsmouth, NH 03801–3912
www.heinemann.com

Offices and agents throughout the world

ISBN-13: 978-0-325-05945-9

Production: Elizabeth Valway, David Stirling, and Abigail Heim
Cover and interior designs: Jenny Jensen Greenleaf
Series includes photographs by Peter Cunningham and Nadine Baldasare
Composition: Publishers' Design and Production Services, Inc.
Manufacturing: Steve Bernier

Printed in the United States of America on acid-free paper
18 17 16 15   VP   2 3 4 5

Contents

Acknowledgments

THIS SERIES is the biggest undertaking of my life—other than the larger projects of leading the Teachers College Reading and Writing Project and of parenting Miles and Evan—and so it is fitting that I dedicate this project to my mother and my father. I thank Evan and Virginia Calkins for all that I am, for all that I believe in, and for giving me eight brothers and sisters—Sally, Steve, Joan, Ben, Hugh, Ellen, Geoff, and Tim—and thirty-some nieces and nephews. Two of the many young people in the extended clan are my sons, Miles and Evan Skorpen. Anyone who has ever read my writing or been part of my teaching knows that the sun rises and sets for me with Miles and Evan. Those of you who have followed their writing through all the years may miss the new infusions of their drafts; they have both become young men now, and I'm not chronicling their comings and goings in quite the same way. John and I could not be more proud of them.

I live and learn as part of the community of teacher-educators that comprises the Teachers College Reading and Writing Project, and all of the people at the Project are my thought-companions. I especially thank Laurie Pessah and Kathleen Tolan, senior deputy directors; Mary Ehrenworth, deputy director for middle school; and Amanda Hartman, associate director. These people are my closest friends, my life partners, and I can't imagine any more beautiful way to work and live than alongside them. I also thank Mary Ann Mustac and the team of fifty-plus full-time staff developers who keep the Project's work vital, robust, and grounded. These people, too, are my partners.

At the desk, my closest partner is Kate Montgomery. Kate and I have imagined, planned, written, and revised all the *Units of Study* series, since their origin. I was only willing to undertake this gigantic all-new Common Core State Standard (CCSS)-aligned effort after Kate agreed to work half-time as essentially the senior coauthor of the entire series. Kate's brilliant mind is ever present in all of these books and in the design of the entire effort.

The ideas about teaching writing that are essential in this book have been evolving since I was a young teacher. Starting then and continuing for years afterward, I worked very closely with two people who opened the field of writing to me and to the world. Other than my parents, Don Graves and Don Murray changed my life more than anyone else. My pathway would have been entirely different had these two incredible mentors not shown me a terrain to explore, given me tools with which to do that exploring, and most of all, empowered me to rise to the occasion.

Words can't easily contain my gratitude to all the coauthors who joined me in writing these books. I thank each individually within the particular books, but some have helped with books beyond their own. Mary Ehrenworth's ideas about middle school teaching have inspired us and given wingspan to all we do. Julia Mooney's impeccable standards and her deep knowledge make her a pillar of strength. Kathleen Tolan's originality and her fearless focus on excellence make her a never-ending source of insight. Kate Roberts took on a yeoman's task of writing not just one but two books, and her efforts have been significant. Kelly Boland Hohne's searing intelligence has left many of us feeling breathless—and blessed. Jenny Bender has contributed steadily to these books, bringing her knowledge of middle schools, of teaching, and of writing to help when the writing burden became especially heavy. Janet Steinberg's hand on the pulse of teacher effectiveness, curricular mapping, Depth of Knowledge (DOK), and the CCSS has kept us all hopping. Audra

Kirshbaum Robb has made us smarter in the arena of performance assessments and in writing about reading. Many school principals have opened their doors to us—none more often than Anael Alston, Alyse Barr, Eileen Brett, Aracelis Castellano-Folkes, David Densieski, Sonhando Estwick, Dawn Faraj, Mark Federman, Ellen Foote, Stacy Goldstein, Ramón González, Claire Lowenstein, Marc Marin, Deanna Sinito, Jennifer Spalding, Mia Williams, and Kenneth Zapata. Peter Cunningham, the photographer for every book I've ever written, graced this effort with magical talent. In this series, we have also used the beautiful and evocative photographs of Nadine Baldasare.

Abby Heim worked together with Kate Montgomery to lead Heinemann's involvement with this effort, and I thank them both for channeling enormous support toward this project. The two of them have kept their hands on the pulse of the entire enterprise, managing the people, the texts, and the dates, and, above all, bringing a knack for structure and knowledge of the project to their marvelous editing efforts. Abby Heim has also been the production mastermind at Heinemann. She and her colleagues Elizabeth Valway, David Stirling, and Shannon Thorner have kept track of all the zillions of bits and pieces that create the mosaic of these books, and done so with a combination of strength, resolve, and focus that keeps everyone's attention on the job at hand. Abby has also been the emotional leader of the enterprise, bringing maturity and experience to that role. Meanwhile, two wonderful new editors joined us as this project was getting underway—Tracy Wells and Karen Kawaguchi—and both have worked with meticulous care. This entire team works under the direction of Lesa Scott, who is at the helm of Heinemann, and I thank her for recognizing the significance of this effort and devoting resources and talent to it. Vicky Boyd, Senior Vice President for Editorial, has also been a stalwart advocate and visionary for the series. Charles McQuillen and Buzz Rhodes take over once Abby and Kate let go, and I thank them in advance for what they and their sales and marketing team of experts will do to usher the books into the hands of teachers.

Most of all, I am grateful to Kate Montgomery, who is my writing partner and co-leader of this entire effort. Kate and I imagined the series together, made the hard decisions together, devised the principles and structures that unify the series together, and supported the coauthors together. It has been a great joy to share responsibility for authoring the ideas and the books in the series with Kate. Her writing embodies the crystal clarity and the warmth that E. B. White describes in his *Elements of Style* (1999). Her knowledge of teaching and literacy research has grown from a lifetime of work with many of the best thinkers in the field. How blessed this project has been to have her constant and close involvement.

A Note to My Readers

IN A MOMENT, I'm going to ask that you step with me into this series, into this world of writing plans and teaching strategies and exciting new ideas for fostering developmental breakthroughs in young writers. In some ways I think of this project as the culmination of my life work so far; it grows from decades of think tanks and teaching and coaching and studying with my colleagues and with teachers from around the world. It represents not only my best work but also the best work of more than fifteen of my colleagues. Here, then, is the grand unveiling of this master work, and I am so eager to share it with you!

Nonetheless, I want to ask you to stop for a moment before you read on. Before you turn to the ins and outs of curriculum and the face of education today, to new standards and best practices, pause for a moment to picture the face of a young person you teach. One young someone you know well. When you see her, stopping by your classroom, sitting backward on a chair, leaning in to talk, does it make you smile? When you picture him, walking slowly away with his head down, backpack slumped over his shoulder, do you want to reach out, maybe call him back? And when you think of all of them, their quirky, tousled, grubby, intent faces looking up at you, I know you feel the tug in your chest, that tug of feeling we are so responsible for them all. We feel it deeply. And this is what I want to say: *that* is the core of all that matters in teaching. Without that care, the greatest curriculum in the world is only paper and a little dry ink.

Chapter 1

A New Mission for Schools and Educators

"The new mission . . . is to get all students to meet high standards of education and to provide them with a lifelong education that does not have built-in obsolescence of so much old-style curriculum but that equips them to be lifelong learners."

—Michael Fullan, Peter Hill, and Carmel Crévola, *Breakthrough*

I N A WORLD that is increasingly dominated by big corporations and big money, it is easy for individuals to feel silenced. No one is more apt to be silenced than young people, who too often grow up being taught to listen rather than to speak out, to be obedient rather than to be critical. The teaching of writing can change that. In a democracy, we must help young people grow up to know how to voice their ideas, to speak out for what is right and good.

The information age of today makes it especially imperative that young people, not just an elite few but all students, develop skills that are significantly more complex than those required of them in the past. In part, the increased focus on writing comes from the technological revolution that has transformed our lives. As the ways of communicating—text messaging, email, social media, search engines—seep into every nook and cranny of our day, all of us are writing more than ever. Today, it has become increasingly important for all students to be given an education that enables them to synthesize, organize, reflect on, and respond to the data in their world. Indeed, several years ago, the National Commission on Writing called for a "writing revolution," suggesting that students needed to double the amount of time they spent writing in their classrooms. They need to be able to write not only narratives but also to write arguments and information texts. They need not only to record information and ideas but also to synthesize, analyze, compare, and contrast that information and those ideas.

In their important book, *Breakthrough* (2006), Michael Fullan, Peter Hill, and Carmel Crévola point out that the old mission for schools used to be to provide universal access to basic education and then to provide a small, elite group entry to a university education. Although that mission may have made sense in the world of our parents, it no longer makes sense. Whereas twenty years ago 95% of jobs were low skilled, today those jobs only constitute 10% of our entire economy (Darling-Hammond et al., *Powerful Learning: What We Know about Teaching for Understanding*, 2008). Students who leave school today without strong literacy skills will no longer find a job waiting for them. "The new mission . . . is to get *all* students to meet high standards of education and to provide them with a lifelong education that does not have built-in obsolescence of so much old-style curriculum but that equips them to be lifelong learners." These words are from the prelude to *Breakthrough*, but they could also appear on the opening page of this book.

As this nation wakes up to the fact that the education millions of Americans received in the past simply isn't adequate for today, more and more schools are realizing that one of the most potent ways to accelerate students' progress as learners is by equipping them with first-rate skills in writing. While the teaching of writing had no place in the No Child Left Behind (NCLB) standards of yesteryear, there has been an about-face since then, and the Common Core State Standards give as much attention to writing as they give to reading—and even suggest that students' abilities to read will be assessed through their abilities to write.

For teachers, parents, and students in schools that have not taught writing in the past, the exemplar student writing showcased in Appendix C of the Common Core (and described by the standards themselves that detail what all students are now expected to know and be able to do) may feel like pie in the sky. I've seen teachers guffaw at some of the samples of writing included in the Common Core as if that work represents an utterly inaccessible goal. That's not a surprising response from educators who have not, themselves, received help teaching writing.

What we now know about writing development is that students need extensive opportunities to write on topics they care about or learn to care about, they need explicit and sequenced instruction that helps them develop

> *"One of the most potent ways to accelerate students' progress as learners is by equipping them with first-rate skills in writing."*

along a learning progression, and they need critical feedback that helps them know next steps. It's a tall order for teachers to provide those conditions to students if they themselves have only received minimal instruction in writing.

But the good news is that the student samples in the appendix of the Common Core are representative of what many students have been doing for a long time. Educators need not feel empty-handed when they ask, "How can we begin to approach the Common Core expectations in writing?" Instead, there are schools across the country that have traveled a good portion of that journey and can help other schools get started. Although many school leaders are just now waking up to the importance of teaching writing, many of us across the nation have had those concerns at heart for a long time. At the Teachers College Reading and Writing Project, for example, we have been working for three decades to develop, pilot, revise, and implement state-of-the-art curriculum in writing. We have had a chance to do this work under the influence of the Common Core for the past few years, and this series—this treasure chest of experiences, theories, techniques, tried-and-true methods, and questions—will bring the results of that work to you.

THIS SERIES: GROWTH FOR STUDENTS AND TEACHERS

This series was born out of a need. In states across the country, elementary school students have been taught with an earlier, very different version of this series. Those students have entered middle school, wanting and expecting to continue their studies as writers. Over the years, thousands of middle school teachers have risen to this challenge, drawing on their own strong literacy skills, on the field of writing process education, and on whatever they can learn from the Teachers College Reading and Writing Project to construct their own improvised writing curriculum. That curriculum has already given young people extraordinary power not only as writers but also as thinkers, learners, and readers. When young people are explicitly taught the craft of proficient writing, they are able to travel the world as writers, applying their skills to discipline-based learning and to their lives . . . and all of this creates quite a stir. As a result, school districts have asked for more—more professional development for middle school teachers in the teaching of writing, and more curricular support materials to help middle school teachers rise to the challenge.

The work has spread from one district to another as school districts find that when teachers receive the education they deserve in the teaching of writing, those teachers are able to provide students with clear, sequenced, vibrant writing instruction (along with opportunities to write often for their own important purposes), and this makes a dramatic difference in young people's abilities to write. Powerful writing instruction produces visible and immediate results; the stories, petitions, speeches, and essays that students produce become far more substantial, complex and significant, revealing the young authors' ideas in ways that make parents, community members, and the students themselves sit up and take notice.

When I work with teachers, I often say to them, "If your students' writing skills are not visibly, dramatically improving after a few weeks of instruction, you are doing something wrong." Over all these years, it has become crystal clear to us that when teaching writing, good teaching pays off. When you provide students with constant opportunities to write and when you actively and assertively teach into their best efforts, their development as writers will astonish you, their parents, the school administrators, and best of all, the students themselves.

It is not only *students'* work that is transformed when teachers are supported in the teaching of writing; *teachers'* work is also transformed. One of the beautiful things about teaching writing is that no one needs to make a choice between responsive, student-centered teaching and results-oriented, data-based teaching. The good news is that when young people write, their thinking, their progress, their vulnerabilities will inevitably be right there before your eyes—and before their eyes, too. Whereas reading must be translated into something that is no longer reading for it to be assessed in black and white, growth in writing is always concrete and demonstrable.

Then, too, when a community of teachers embraces reform in the teaching of writing, teachers often become reinvigorated and renewed in the process. And individual teachers find that teaching writing taps new sources of energy within themselves. Over the years, teachers have repeatedly told me that the teaching of writing has given them new energy, clarity, and compassion, reminding them why they went into teaching in the first place. I understand what these teachers mean, for writing has done all this—and more—for me as well.

All of this creates an escalating demand for professional development in writing. This series aims to meet that demand—to provide professional development in a box!

THIS SERIES: BOTH CURRICULUM *AND* PROFESSIONAL DEVELOPMENT

The *Units of Study in Argument, Information, and Narrative Writing* series has been written in a way that it doubles as both curricular support and professional development. Each day's instruction is designed according to research-based principles. For example, you will see that in one day after another, all of the teaching follows the "gradual release of responsibility" model of teaching. Students first learn from a demonstration (accompanied by an explicit explanation), then from guided practice in which the amount of scaffolding they receive lessens over time, and then from independent work, for which they receive feedback. Then, too, when we first use a new method, the method itself is a simplified and streamlined version of something that becomes more complex and nuanced over time. Over time, the method becomes more layered and complex, more fluid and implicit.

The progressions that you will see in our teaching are always carefully chosen and explicitly explained. Our goal is not just to provision you with a coherent, principled curriculum, but also to teach you to teach writing *and* to invent your own teaching. Throughout any unit, we highlight the replicable teaching decisions and moves in ways that allow you to transfer those same decisions and moves to curriculum that you invent. Because my colleagues and I have spent thirty years helping hundreds of thousands of teachers learn to teach writing, and because we have studied that work, reflecting on it as we engage in a continual process of revision, we know a lot about how to teach teachers to teach writing—and that is the aim of this series. While the units scaffold your teaching, they also help you develop finesse and flexibility to invent other units, and to transfer this teaching to other disciplines.

The wonderful thing about learning to teach writing well is that there are just a few teaching methods that one needs to know and be able to use. In this series, I provide crystal clear advice on how to lead efficient and effective minilessons, conferences, and small-group strategy sessions. I do so knowing that as you travel through the series, encountering scores of examples of minilessons, conferences, small-group sessions, and shares, you will learn not only from explicit instruction but also from immersion. This—the first book of the series—explicitly describes the architecture of all our minilessons, conferences, and small-group strategy sessions, and it details the management techniques that make writing workshops possible. *Writing Pathways: Performance Assessments and Learning Progressions, Grades 6–8* provides you with an assessment system that can make teaching and learning robust, goal directed, data based, and responsive. The unit books show these methods and principles affecting real-life classrooms.

Ideally, you and every other teacher in the world should be able not only to observe exemplary teaching but also to do so with a coach nearby, highlighting the way the teaching puts into action a collection of guiding principles. Therefore, as you witness my teaching and that of my colleagues, I will also be an ever-present coach, underscoring aspects of the teaching that seem especially essential. My goal is to enable you to extrapolate guidelines and methods as you watch this teaching, so that on another day you'll begin to invent your own teaching. After all, these books provide a detailed model; but they are *not* a script. The end goal is not the teaching that we've described here but the teaching that you, your colleagues, and your students invent together.

AN OVERVIEW OF THE SERIES

This one book—*A Guide to the Common Core Writing Workshop*—accompanies the series of books written for sixth-grade teachers, for seventh-grade teachers, and also for eighth-grade teachers. (I've also written a similar guide for K–2 and 3–5 teachers.) For middle school, each grade's series contains:

- The *Guide to the Common Core Writing Workshop*
- Three Common Core–aligned units of study, including one unit each in argument, information, and narrative writing, though in some instances the units are hybrids of these kinds of writing, as writing in the world tends to be
- A book of alternate and additional units, *If . . . Then . . . Curriculum*, written to help you differentiate curriculum as well as supplement the three units of study provided
- *Writing Pathways: Performance Assessments and Learning Progressions*, a book that puts a system for assessing writing into your hands and into the hands of your students

- A CD-ROM, *Resources for Teaching Writing*, of additional resources, including sample student writing, reproducible checklists, some mentor texts, and Web links

The intent of this series is to support students' abilities to be strategic, metacognitive writers who use particular processes to achieve particular purposes. Within a grade and across grades, the books fit tongue-and-groove alongside each other. Together, they help students consolidate and use what they have learned so that they meet and exceed the Common Core State Standards for each grade. More importantly, the books help students learn to use writing as a tool for learning across the day and throughout their richly literate lives.

Three Units of Study Books

Each unit of study book represents about five weeks of teaching. Sometimes, within those five weeks, the unit supports several cycles of drafting, revision, and publication, and other times the unit takes students through one, in-depth cycle. The units align roughly with the three types of writing specified in the Common Core State Standards, although by eighth grade, the distinctions between the units blur. (Is a unit on journalism *narrative* writing or is it *argument*—or *information*? Are the units on writing about literature *information*—or *argument*? Of course, as genres in the world will be, these kinds of writing are a blend of narrative, information, and argument!) However, at each grade level, one of the unit of study books falls mostly within the progression of one of the kinds of writing. For example, in the progression of argument writing, students in sixth grade first write literary essays, including a compare-and-contrast essay, in which they support their arguments about the literature they have read closely. Next, in seventh grade, students write petitions, persuasive letters, and argument essays within a unit that begins with an exploration into the pros and cons of competitive sports. In eighth grade, students build on their skills in writing literary essays, now arguing for their claims about short stories in more sophisticated and complex ways. Eighth-graders also spend an entire unit writing analytical position papers, first explaining and then arguing for their point of view on a complex, globally significant topic. In this same way, there are also progressions of units supporting students' development in both narrative and information writing.

The unit books are written to give you the opportunity to listen in on and observe the unit being taught with students just the age of your students. It will seem as if you were invited into a classroom to watch and listen as my coauthors and I teach and work with young people. You will listen as we convene the class for a ten-minute minilesson, channeling the students to work with partners, calling for their attention, and you'll hear how we talk about and demonstrate the strategies and skills of effective writing. Of course, you'll also overhear the jokes and stories we use to draw them in and the directions we give to send them off to their work time. Then, too, you'll hear the ways we confer and lead small groups to support the work students do during that day's workshop. You'll watch us teach writers to self-assess their writing early in a unit of study, becoming familiar with goals for that unit, and you'll see the way that learning progressions and data weave through every unit of study. You'll also see pre- and postassessments bookend each unit of study.

Each of the three units of study books contains the words of our teaching (and students' responses to it) for that entire five-week-long unit of study. We also provide representative examples of the writing young people did in each unit of study.

Once you begin teaching a unit, you will find that each day's teaching—each *session*—within that unit is introduced with a prelude that helps you to understand why, out of all that could possibly be taught at that juncture, we decided on that particular minilesson. The art of teaching comes from choice. The prelude, then, brings you in on the rationale behind the choices that inform the upcoming session. Why this minilesson? How will it fit with earlier and with later instruction? What are the real goals? The prelude highlights what matters most in the session, and hopefully functions as a bit of a keynote speech, revving you up for the teaching that follows.

Then you can listen in to state-of-the-art *minilessons*, taught to students who are just the age of your own. Hear the language that the coauthors and I use, and hear some of the ways students respond. Each minilesson follows the same structure, which is described in more detail in Chapter 7.

After we send students off to their work, my colleagues and I fill you in on the *conferring and small-group work* we think you are apt to do during the work time that day. More often than not, this section will be like a miniature workshop, showing you ways to anticipate the challenges your students are likely to encounter and giving you the opportunity to be ready to teach responsively. That teaching will be punctuated with *mid-workshop teaching* that you will offer to the whole class, part way through writing time. Often this teaching builds on the minilesson, extending it by providing a next step or a follow-up point. Sometimes the mid-workshop teaching counterbalances the minilesson or broadcasts lessons being taught in conferences or small groups. We also describe the whole-class share session that culminates the workshop.

By the time students are in middle school, they can do substantial work at home, and they will be more eager to do this work if you are careful to craft homework that helps them outgrow themselves. Most sessions also contain suggested *homework* assignments.

A Book of Alternate and Additional Units

In addition to the three units of study for each grade level, we have written *If . . . Then . . . Curriculum: Assessment-Based Instruction*. This book offers shortened versions of nine units of study that you might decide to teach before, after, or in between the units we've provided in full. For example, if you worry that your eighth-graders didn't participate in the sixth-grade unit on literary essay writing and they might be missing background skills needed for the eighth-grade unit, this book, *If . . . Then . . . Curriculum*, will coach you to know whether that is a problem and to help you develop some preliminary instruction if it is called for. Similar help is offered if you need to support students who may not be ready for the seventh-grade argument unit. Then again, your students may instead be chomping at the bit for additional challenges, and the *If . . . Then . . . Curriculum* book provides you with plans and help for teaching units in poetry, fantasy, documentaries, and the like. The curriculum we've described in the full-length books only supports a portion of your writing curriculum, so you will want to adapt and use some of these additional units of study.

A Book of Assessment Tools

The curriculum set out in these units is integrated into an assessment system that includes three learning progressions, one in each type of writing, as well as grade-by-grade checklists and grade-specific rubrics. We've also included two benchmark texts illustrating on-demand student writing at standards level for each kind of writing—argument, information, and narrative. An early version of this assessment system has been piloted in thousands of classrooms, and the entire system has been revised based on student, teacher, coach, and administrator feedback.

Essentially, in this system, K–8 teachers begin the school year by asking students to spend forty-five minutes writing an on-demand narrative (and on other days, to spend similar time writing an on-demand information text and argument text). A teacher might say to her students, "You have forty-five minutes to write your best personal narrative, true story, or piece of short fiction—your best narrative. Write in a way that shows me all you know about narrative writing."

Each student's work is then scored against a rubric, built from a learning progression using an accompanying set of sample student texts in each genre that have been benchmarked to represent each level of the learning progression. For example, a scorer can read the introduction in one student's information text, asking, "Does this match expectations for a sixth-grade introduction? A fifth-grade introduction? A seventh-grade one?" Then, teachers teach a unit on information writing, giving students ample opportunities to assess themselves at the beginning, middle, and end of the unit against checklists that spell out the goals they should be working toward. After the unit is completed, the on-demand assessment is repeated, and students' work is again scored. Often teachers will teach more than one unit in each of the three major kinds of writing, in which case the on-demands are given periodically throughout the year to continue to track students' progress.

The most important thing about the learning progressions and performance assessments is that they enable teachers and students alike to grasp where students are in their writing development, so that you can figure out ways to help them move toward next steps. The assessment system that undergirds this curriculum is meant as an instructional tool. It makes progress in writing transparent, concrete, and as obtainable as possible, and puts ownership for this progress into the hands of learners. As part of this, this system of assessment demystifies the Common Core State Standards, allowing students and teachers to work toward a very clear image of what good writing entails.

A CD-ROM of Additional Resources

The accompanying CD-ROM offers student samples, short video clips, Web links, mentor texts, and more resources to go with particular sessions. On the CD-ROM, you'll also find reproducible checklists and rubrics, editing checklists, and conferring scenarios (from the *If . . . Then . . . Curriculum*

book) that can be printed on label paper so you can leave your students with an artifact of your teaching, as well as links to websites that will help you and your students do research for your writing projects. These resources will support your teaching throughout the year.

The Series Components All Together: A PreK–8 Learning Progression

If you are truly going to bring all of your students to the ambitious standards of the CCSS, there needs to be vertical alignment in the curriculum so that people who teach at any one grade level can count on students entering their classrooms with some foundational skills that can then be built upon. The days of each teacher functioning as a Lone Ranger in the teaching of writing are at an end. Imagine how impractical it would be if each sixth-grade math teacher decided whether to introduce ratios to their students: seventh-grade teachers who received students from several different sixth-grade classrooms would find that half the class had no knowledge or vocabulary around ratios, and the other half would be ready, with some review, to move ahead toward solving much more complex ratio problems. Of course, almost every school *does* have a math curriculum that supports vertical alignment. Granted, even in a school where students are all taught ratios in sixth grade, some students won't master those skills; still, there is agreement that a shared math curriculum means that teachers can extend and build on previous instruction. Until the release of the Common Core State Standards, many educators didn't realize that writing skills, too, need to be developed incrementally, with the work that students do at one grade level standing on the shoulders of prior learning.

In this series, instruction builds on itself. Often that instruction may have occurred in a different genre, within that same school year. For example, a teacher might say, "In your earlier unit of study in narrative writing, you learned that there can be tension between what a character says and what that character actually thinks or feels. Today I want to teach you that this insight is important also when writing a research report, because there may be times when you doubt the veracity of a quotation or a statistic." In this way, you bring students to higher levels of achievement by making sure that your teaching stands on the shoulders of prior instruction.

Sometimes the prior instruction that undergirds a minilesson will have occurred during the previous year. "I know that last year, you learned that when writing about information, it helps to try different organizational structures on for size, deciding which one is best for your purposes. This year, I want to let you know it is important to include a few sentences within your introductory paragraph that let readers know the plan for how you will organize the information, for how those subsections will go. Your transition words vary depending on your structure."

Of course, teaching involves not only a well-planned curriculum but also deep assessment and responsive instruction. Students will be able to proceed up the vertical alignment in the series only if you use, and make teaching decisions based on, the assessments in this series. These assessments scaffold the curriculum and are also aligned both to the Common Core State Standards and to the preceding grade levels' work. For example, the CCSS state that in seventh grade, writers must be able to introduce claims, acknowledge alternate or opposing claims, and organize reasons and evidence logically (CCSS ELA-Literacy W.7.1a). When teaching into a standard as complex as the one cited above, it's crucial to know the various kinds of writing work that lead up to this—the invisible foundation that would support students' ability to demonstrate proficiency in this. Using a rubric based on the learning progression for argument writing, teachers can collect data that reveals, for example, which students still need help organizing reasons and evidence logically. In this way, teachers can be specific about where on the learning progression these students' work falls: is it close to seventh-grade work, or more like sixth grade, or fifth grade? Looking back at prior years' checklists can support targeted intervention that will help cement the background skills necessary to moving forward.

The Relationship between This Series and the CCSS

As this book goes to press, the Common Core standards are very much under attack. Michael Fullan has suggested they are the great ship *Titanic*, and are doomed to sink because of a fatal flaw (implementation). The fact that the standards are in contention brings home an important point. No school should reform its writing curriculum because of the Common Core. The CCSS ask schools to do more than any one school will be able to embrace, and ultimately, a school needs to choose its priorities. So reform your writing curriculum because you believe that in today's world, people write as they talk and think and read—all the time. Reform your writing curriculum because you believe that in a democracy, people need to be heard, to have ways to bring their voices to the table. Reform your writing curriculum because doing so will intensify your reading curriculum as students learn in the most firsthand and first-person way possible that writers make choices for deliberate reasons. But don't adopt this curriculum because of the Common Core.

Having said that, you should know that the standards are not just painted like a patina over the surface of these units. First, the CCSS have been important to us. The book I wrote with two colleagues (Ehrenworth and Lehman) is the best-selling book on the CCSS and is listed as #7 in the *New York Times* list of bestselling books on education. My colleagues and I lead a lot of professional development specifically on the standards. We know the CCSS well and find they can provide an important infrastructure into which a curriculum can be developed. The fit was an easy one for us. It seems as if many aspects of the writing standards had been written with a writing workshop precisely in mind. To those of us who know the fingerprints of writing workshop instruction, it is clear that many of the exemplar texts in the appendix emerged from workshops.

The Teachers College Reading and Writing Project did, absolutely, need to develop some new curriculum so as to meet the challenges of the CCSS. In particular, the CCSS challenged us to develop more sequential, ambitious work in opinion/argument writing. We formed a think tank with argument researchers from ETS (Educational Testing Service) and with them, researched learning progressions and curriculum in argument writing. You'll see the results in two of our units.

The Teachers College Reading and Writing Project is especially embedded in schools within New York State, which is a "hard core Common Core" state. This means that the frameworks New York State has adopted for accelerating achievement toward CCSS levels are part and parcel of these units. This includes:

- An emphasis on close reading and text-based questioning
- An emphasis on data-based instruction, and on formative and summative assessments

- Attention to the level of cognitive challenge we provide students using Webb's Depth of Knowledge as a guide

- Reliance on curricular mapping design strategies

- Attention to Charlotte Danielson's teacher-effectiveness framework

The work your students will do as you teach the units of study in this series and as you track and support their progress on the learning progressions that undergird this curriculum will provide them with the instruction, opportunities for practice, and goals they need to meet the CCSS for writing at their grade level. The CCSS for eighth-grade students are high. We believe the best way to be sure students will be able to meet the demands of the eighth-grade standards is for them to enter fifth grade already well on the way toward mastering the sixth-grade standards and, in sixth grade, to push beyond the sixth-grade standards, when possible. The units, then, help teachers and students aim not only for grade-level standards but also beyond them. Runners don't aim to stop at the finish line; they aim to run right through it, keeping up the pace until the finish line is well behind them. We, too, want to aim beyond the finish line—bringing every writer with us as we do so.

Although this series does not take on the entire job of helping students meet the Common Core Reading, Speaking and Listening, and Language Standards, good writing instruction requires meeting many of these standards all the same, and you'll find the units help you do this. You'll see CCSS correlation charts aligned to each unit that will help you understand which of these other sets of standards these units help you meet and which will especially need attention in other times of the school day—in social studies or science, reading, and language/word study. The good news is that the work students do across the entire curriculum will be given a lift by the skills they develop within the writing workshop.

I discuss the CCSS in more depth in the next chapter.

The Relationship between This Series and Teacher-Effectiveness Work

Since we published the first *Units of Study in Opinion, Information, and Narrative Writing* series, knowledge of education has changed. The work of Danielson, Marzano, Webb, and others has coalesced into new images and understandings of effective practice. Teachers are being assessed with new lenses in mind. Many of the schools we know best have especially adopted the Danielson Frameworks for Teaching (FfT), and this means that her thinking has been combed through all of these lessons. Readers wanting more specific help aligning the FfT with these units will want to look at the Teachers College Reading and Writing Project website for more help aligning the two frameworks. You'll see guides to observing writing workshops with the Danielson lens in hand, advice on how best to be marked as a distinguished teacher when leading writing workshops, suggestions for ramping up aspects of your teaching that are especially prized by FfT, and videotapes of full-length writing workshops with a pre- and postconference, and with low inference notes included.

Other new lenses and emphases have been woven into these units of study as well. You'll see close reading, text-based questions, high levels of Depth of Knowledge, and so forth. That is, over the past decades, the Teachers College Reading and Writing Project has been a major vehicle for professional development in more than a thousand schools, including high-need schools and high-performing private, charter, and public schools. These partnerships mean that we have regularly helped schools undergo quality review, develop and adopt CCSS-aligned performance assessments, use software systems to track student progress, and demonstrate to evaluators that instruction is data-based and differentiated. Our deep involvement with all of this work has helped our own ideas evolve. The fruits of that labor are infused into these units of study.

THE AUTHORSHIP OF THIS SERIES

Although the text reads as if one teacher created and taught the minilessons, mid-workshop teachings, small groups, and shares, the creation and teaching was actually much more collaborative. Usually, before embarking on a project, scores of units of study related to the topic of the unit book will have been piloted. Once we got closer to the work of actually setting the units onto the page, the work usually began with the coauthor and me working hard to develop a tentative plan for the entire unit. Implicit in such a document are literally hundreds of decisions, and our initial plans were always revised endlessly before becoming the backbone of the unit. Part of that revision process involved passing the plans among many of us because the units that we write will become essential to all the Teachers College

Reading and Writing Project's work in schools, and we all needed to agree with the major decisions.

During the early planning portion of the process, we'd decide on mentor texts, the number of cycles through the writing process, and on the bends of the unit. Then one of us would draft a minilesson or two, and that minilesson would be placed on Google Docs so that we could all work with it. The lesson would be revised, piloted, revised again, and principles from that revision would go out from the work with that one minilesson to all coauthors of all the books. "Just a note to remember that it helps to . . . ."

I am the coauthor on some books, and on those books I played a very major writing role. On the other books, for which I am an editor, I played a different role; more of coaching, revising, rewriting, problem spotting, and problem solving. No matter what, however, the initial draft of the first bend went through four or five wholesale revisions, was taught several times, and was passed among a number of hands before it was close to being finished.

Once the first bend had been written and taught, plans for the upcoming bend would be revised based on all that we'd learned, and then the process continued. At least half the books were revised from head to toe even after we thought they were nearly finished based on our work in classrooms.

In the same way, although the books read as if they draw on one classroom, depicting the true story of how that unit of study unfolded in that one classroom, in truth, the classroom depicted in these books is usually a composite classroom, and the kids' voices are captured or created from all of the kids we've taught.

The series, then, stands on the shoulders of the Teachers College Reading and Writing Project community. The books have, in a sense, been coauthored by the entire staff of this professional development organization and by the students, teachers, principals, and superintendents who have become part of the community of practice, helping develop, pilot, and revise the ideas that fill the pages of these books.

Chapter 2

What Do the CCSS Say about Writing, and What Does This Mean for Us?

THIS SERIES IS BEING PUBLISHED just as the United States sets out on an effort to lift the level of literacy instruction across all our schools, making sure that students enter college and twenty-first-century careers ready to flourish. As I've written in what is now the best-selling book nationwide on the CCSS, *Pathways to the Common Core* (2012), the Common Core State Standards are a big deal. Adopted by forty-five states and the District of Columbia so far, the standards represent the most sweeping reform of the K–12 curriculum that has ever occurred in this country. It is safe to say that across the entire history of American education, no single document has played a more influential role over what is taught in our schools. The standards are already shaping what is published, mandated, and tested in schools—and also what is marginalized and neglected. Any educator who wants to play a role in shaping what happens in schools, therefore, needs a deep understanding of these standards.

One of the most striking features of the Common Core State Standards is their tremendous emphasis on writing. In effect, the standards refocus the nation on students' proficiency as writers. NCLB, the last large-scale reform movement in literacy, called for an emphasis on phonemic awareness, phonics, vocabulary, fluency, and comprehension; writing was nowhere in the picture. In the Common Core State Standards, in contrast, writing is treated as an equal partner to reading, and more than this, writing is assumed to be *the* vehicle through which a great deal of the critical thinking, reading work, and reading assessment will occur. Three of the ten reading standards require that students read like writers, noticing the craft decisions the author has made and thinking about the purposes for those decisions. The CCSS, then, return writing to its place as one of the essentials of education.

In this chapter, I lay out the specifics of the Common Core's call for writing instruction and show how these units of study help you meet (and even, at times, exceed) these demands. This chapter looks specifically at:

- The standards' emphasis on three types of writing
- The relationship between the CCSS for writing and the *Units of Study in Argument, Information, and Narrative Writing* series
- The writing process described in the standards and taught in these units of study
- The standards' call for new levels of proficiency

In subsequent chapters in this guide, you'll see how the structure, focus, and content of the units align to—and are influenced by—the Common Core State Standards. You'll see the influence of the Common Core also as you read the individual lessons that lead students toward and beyond CCSS benchmarks.

THE STANDARDS' EMPHASIS ON THREE TYPES OF WRITING

In the prelude to the Common Core Standards, there is a section titled "Key Features of the Standards." This synopsis emphasizes that although the writing process applies to all kinds of writing, different types of writing place different demands on students. We agree.

The standards are organized in a way that highlights grade-specific expectations for three broad types of writing. The first standard delineates expectations for opinion and argument writing; the second, for information writing; and the third, for narrative writing. Although these three standards represent just under a third of the ten standards, if one were to count the pages devoted to the writing standards and count the pages devoted to explicating the three types of writing, one would find that these first three standards occupy fully half of the CCSS for writing. (The later standards illuminate how students should do the work of the first three standards. For example, students presumably will use the writing process detailed in Standard 5, the Writing Process Standard, as they write the argument, information, and narrative texts described in Standards 1–3.)

It is interesting to note that the standards refer to these as *types* of writing and not as *genres*. This makes sense because within any one type of writing, one can lodge many different genres of writing. In the New Standards Project, an earlier effort to create nationwide standards, the committee of twenty (including me) who wrote those standards wrestled with the issue of *kinds* versus *structures* versus *types* versus *genres* of writing and came to the decision that the whole world of writing could be divided into five (not three) *kinds* of writing: narrative, information, functional and procedural, persuasion and argument, and poetry. The Common Core State Standards' divisions are roughly in line with those earlier ones, although functional and procedural writing are now combined with information writing, and poetry is excluded.

You might, with colleagues, try jotting down the genres you would put under these major categories, and then consider how often your students have opportunities to engage in each of the three main types of writing. You will probably come up with lists like these.

- **Narrative writing:** personal narrative, fiction, historical fiction, fantasy, narrative memoir, biography, narrative nonfiction
- **Persuasive/opinion/argument writing:** persuasive letter, petition, persuasive speech, review, personal essay, persuasive essay, literary essay, historical essay, editorial, op-ed column, research-based argument essay
- **Informational and functional/procedural writing:** how-to book, directions, recipe, lab report, fact sheet, news article, feature article, blog, website, report, analytic memo, research report, nonfiction book

The CCSS and Narrative Writing

Although the sequence of the first three anchor standards for writing starts with argument writing and ends with narrative writing, learners grow into these genres in just the opposite direction. Human beings grow up on narratives, on stories. We come to know our own parents by hearing their stories of growing up. We make friendships by sharing the stories of our lives. We get jobs and scholarships by telling the stories of our studies and careers. We stay in touch by regaling each other with the news of our comings and goings. We plan and daydream and work and worry in narrative; we recall and remember in narrative. We comprehend fiction and biography and narrative nonfiction by synthesizing what we read on one page, another, and another into narratives that we hope are coherent and satisfying.

Narratives are important not only because they are, as researcher Barbara Hardy says, the primary mode of knowing ("Narrative as a Primary Act of Mind," in *The Cool Web: The Patterns of Students' Reading*, 1977) but also because they are an essential component in almost every other kind of writing. Listen to TED (Technology, Entertainment, Design) talks—models of persuasive and informative speaking—and you will find that mostly, those speeches are mosaics of stories. Read a terrific informational text, and you'll find that you are reading stories.

If you try to understand the narrative writing standards by turning immediately to the grade you teach and reading the descriptors for that grade, you'll probably find the expectations are overwhelming. Before you dismiss the standards as unrealistically high, you need to read them in an entirely different fashion. Start with kindergarten, and read those grade-level skills for narrative. Imagine a very simple story that meets those descriptors. Then reread just the first subitem in the kindergarten narrative standard before looking to the right to note what added work first-graders are expected to do in narrative writing. The added work won't be much—and that will prove true as you progress through the narrative expectations. By proceeding in this way, reading in a horizontal fashion, setting the descriptors for each skill from one grade alongside those for the next grade and noting the new work that is added at each subsequent grade, you'll come to understand the trajectory along which writers can travel. It is this trajectory that we used when designing the narrative units in this series (and it is the information and argument trajectories that we used for the information and argument units). Using these incremental steps, this steady progression will, in fact, make the writing standards something that students can achieve, especially if they have the opportunity to grow up within a strong writing curriculum.

The CCSS and Opinion/Argument Writing

Argument writing is a *big deal* in the Common Core State Standards. In fact, the writers include an entire section in Appendix A titled "The Special Place of Argument in the Standards" to emphasize their strong belief in argumentation. The section begins: "While all three text types are important, the Standards put particular emphasis on students' ability to write sound

arguments on substantive topics and issues, as this ability is critical to college and career readiness" (2010, 24). To support their argument, the authors refer to statements by college professors who each make additional claims for the centrality of argument in universities. Gerald Graff, for example, claims that the university is largely "an argument culture" (*Clueless in Academe*, 2003, 24). It is with this particular vision of university life that the standards writers mapped their expectations for argument writing from high school graduation backward.

This belief in the essential nature of argumentation, at least on the part of the writers of the standards, comes through in many areas of the CCSS document. There is a push for logical reasoning, analysis of claims, and reliance on clear evidence and evaluation of sources throughout the document.

There are three important ideas that will help you study the Common Core standards for argument writing: the progression of expectations for opinion and argument writing is steep; the K–5 emphasis on opinion writing gives way to a 6–12 emphasis on argument writing (which includes counterargument and more critical weighing of sources, evidence, and logic); and writing arguments eventually includes using and evaluating sources, and using this analysis to power convincing arguments.

The CCSS and Information Writing

To understand the Common Core State Standards for information writing, it is helpful to pause for a moment and think of all the information writing that students do in school. Although research reports and nonfiction books spring to mind right away, this category of writing is far broader than that. Information writing includes entries, Post-it® notes, summaries written in response to reading, lab reports, math records, and descriptions of and reflections on movies, field trips, and books. Under the umbrella of the broad category, one also finds the answers students write in response to questions at the end of textbook chapters or questions discussed in class. The CCSS authors highlight the breadth of this type of writing in Appendix A.

Informational/explanatory writing includes a wide array of genres, including academic genres such as literary analyses, scientific and historical reports, summaries, and précis writing as well as forms of workplace and functional writing such as instructions, manuals, memos, reports, applications, and résumés. (23)

In essence, the skills required to write information texts are not just writing skills, they are learning skills. Let's clarify something before diving much further into this topic: although the rhetoric around the Common Core suggests that the standards call for exponentially increasing the amount of information writing done in school, this depends on the amount of writing teachers have done all along. The truth is that the Common Core standards ask only that just over one third of all the writing that students do *across the entire day* be information writing. That is, most of the writing in science, social studies, art, and computers all qualifies as information writing. This may not, in fact, be an ambitious expectation.

We think it's important to note that for many schools, the challenge is not that students must begin to devote a greater percentage of their writing time to texts that fall under the broad umbrella of information writing (it is already commonplace for one third of the writing that students do to be information writing). Rather, the challenge is that the Common Core expects students to apply the same standard of craftsmanship to information writing as they do to short stories, memoirs, and essays. That is, traditionally, when students wrote about reading (whether literature or history or science), the goal was for them to show that they had done the reading, gleaned the necessary knowledge, and developed some thoughts. Prior to the arrival of the CCSS, it wasn't typical for their information writing to be held up to the same standards as essays and short stories. Now, a reader of the CCSS can quickly see that across all three kinds of writing, there is a parallel emphasis on writing in clear structures, on elaborating with specific information, on writing with details and examples, and on synthesizing the text so that the entire text advances key ideas or themes.

THE RELATIONSHIP BETWEEN THE CCSS FOR WRITING AND THE UNITS OF STUDY IN OPINION/ARGUMENT, INFORMATION, AND NARRATIVE WRITING SERIES

The standards, you'll recall, focus on expectations and not methods. They detail what students should know and be able to do, and they do not specify practices that teachers must use to teach students the skills necessary to meet those expectations. School districts and teachers are left to decide on an instructional program that will elevate the level of student writing so that all (or most) students reach these ambitious expectations. Any effort to meet the standards will require a planned, sequential, explicit writing curriculum, with instruction that gives students repeated opportunities to practice each kind of writing and to receive explicit feedback at frequent intervals.

This new series offers one such curriculum. Contained within this series is a unit devoted to each type of writing at each grade level, although a few units are hybrid, allowing there to sometimes be two units supporting one kind of writing in one year. Within any unit of study, students are expected to write more than one piece (and sometimes a multitude of pieces) representing that kind of writing. The fact that students are given repeated opportunities to produce a particular kind of writing is important if we are going to hold students accountable to meeting CCSS expectations. For anyone to become highly skilled at a specific type of writing, that person needs opportunities for repeated practice.

Progression and Transference across Units and Grades

Across all of the units, there is a continual emphasis on transference. For example, after students write literary essays, they study another kind of essay writing—research-based argument essays—and ask, "What learning can I take from that work to apply to this work?" This transference leads students to plunge right into the work of writing argument essays without needing another elaborate introduction. This series promotes transference also as students go from writing personal narratives to writing fiction and from fiction to narrative journalism. The very design of the Common Core emphasizes the fact that students are able to reach high-level expectations because skills are built on and developed through a cross-grade progression. In this series, the cohesion across units means that skills that are introduced in one grade level are then recalled and developed in later units of study and in subsequent years.

This development occurs within a type of writing and also across the full spectrum of writing. That is, the standards' expectations for one type of writing, at a grade level, are echoed in the other two types of writing. If students are expected to end their essays by referring back not only to the last paragraph but to their entire essay, they'll encounter parallel expectations for their endings when writing narratives and information texts. It is helpful for students when teachers say, "You know the work you have been doing to make sure that the ending of your essay relates to the whole text, not just to the last bit of it? Well, when you write fiction, there are similar expectations for your endings. Let me explain and show you what I mean . . ."

You will want to study the standards so that you understand the way that expectations grow each year, with students being expected to produce work that stands on the shoulders of the preceding year. For example, first-graders are expected to write opinion pieces in which they introduce the topic they are writing about, state an opinion, supply a reason to support that opinion, and provide some sense of closure. By sixth grade, students are expected to write arguments (not opinions) to support claims with clear reasons and relevant evidence. In these arguments, students are expected to introduce the claim(s) and organize the reasons and evidence clearly; support claim(s) with clear reasons and relevant evidence; use credible sources to demonstrate an understanding of the topic or text; use words, phrases, and clauses to clarify the relationships among claims and reasons; establish a formal style; and provide a concluding statement or section that follows from the argument presented. By eighth grade, students must also distinguish between their claims and alternate or opposing claims, use logical reasoning to support their claims, and determine the relevance and validity of a variety of sources, including explaining when a source seems problematic or misleading.

The standards not only describe the progression of skill development expected to occur across grades in a curriculum in which one grade builds on the next, but they also provide annotated exemplar texts to illustrate what these pieces of writing might look like and to answer the question, "How good is good enough?" When looking at the pieces provided as illustrations of one type of writing or another, it is important to note that even the pieces selected as exemplars do not adhere to all of the defining characteristics of a genre. For readers who are accustomed to teaching in writing workshops, it will be clear after just a glance that most of the exemplar pieces in Appendix B emerged out of writing workshop classrooms.

Exemplar pieces are important, and although the standards include a random sampling of some exemplars, they don't show information, opinion, and narrative pieces that illustrate each of the standards they detail. This series does provide those benchmark texts in *Writing Pathways: Performance Assessments and Learning Progressions*. Of course, once you teach these units, you will have files of student work from previous years that you can draw on, and you will want to do so.

If you are teaching in isolation, a lone champion of writing in your school, I encourage you to reach out in every possible way to your colleagues. Your influence on one class of writers will be multiplied tenfold if students receive continual instruction in writing during subsequent years and if they are asked to transfer and apply their skills across the curriculum. To reach the Common Core standards, students benefit from writing becoming a schoolwide vision.

Writing across the Curriculum

The CCSS emphasize that writing needs to occur in disciplines and be supported by all teachers. Writing cannot be the province only of the language arts classroom. As part of this, the CCSS spotlight the importance of high standards for writing that is done within the content areas. Students need to be able to structure their research reports, synthesize information, and explore the ramifications of evidence across all disciplines. This means that young people need explicit instruction and lots of opportunities to write within social studies and science, and to develop as writers of information and argument texts. Two thirds of the units in this series revolve around source-based writing, with half of those being writing about fiction, and half, nonfiction.

A word about balance. The standards not only define and describe the three kinds of writing and show how students' work within each of those kinds of writing should progress across the years, but they also call for a distribution of writing experiences that gives students roughly equal amounts of time and instruction in argument, informative, and narrative writing. Sometimes this mandate has been misunderstood to suggest that two thirds of the English Language Arts (ELA) writing curriculum (or half the ELA reading curriculum)

"To reach the Common Core standards, students benefit from writing becoming a schoolwide vision."

should revolve around information texts. The mandate actually pertains to a student's entire day, and not just to ELA time.

It is important to point out that in the Common Core, the discussion of the distribution of writing between the types of texts is situated under the subheading of "Shared Responsibility" as part of an emphasis on writing instruction belonging in the hands of all disciplines and every teacher. So, if eighth-grade students are expected to write to persuade (argument) 35% of the time, to explain (informational) 35% of the time, and to convey experience (narrative) 30% of the time, the balance between the three types of writing is expected to occur across math, social studies, science, gym, and music, as well as during writing workshop itself. Presumably, a good deal of the information writing will occur in science (lab reports), in math (math journals reflecting on the students' processes), in social studies (summaries of texts read, responses to questions asking students to synthesize information from several sources), and in reading (reading notebook entries, quick analytic jottings, preparations for partnership, and book club conversations).

The implications of the writing standards are clear. Instruction in writing must become part of the Bill of Rights for all students. In the world of the Common Core, it is indefensible for a teacher of any subject to say, "Writing is not really my cup of tea."

THE WRITING PROCESS DESCRIBED IN THE STANDARDS AND TAUGHT IN THESE UNITS OF STUDY

While there is some dispute in this nation about methods for teaching *reading*, there is less dispute about methods for teaching *writing*. This is probably because while we don't have many public figures who are readers, there have been thousands of writers who have made their process public. There is near universal agreement that writers engage in a process of collecting, drafting, revising, and editing. You can see writers' drafts, with their many revisions, in library collections, online, and in books such as the Author at Work series. From Mark Twain to Bob Woodward, from novelists to journalists, writers draft and revise—sometimes rapidly and on the run, and sometimes over extended periods. It's no surprise, then, that the standards embrace the widely accepted writing process.

Writing Standard 5 describes the writing process, and Standard 10 describes the need to write routinely as part of that process. Both standards are an integral part of attaining all the other writing standards as well as ends in and of themselves. The grade-level specifics of anchor Standard 5 are almost the same across all the grades. This standard says that students should be able to "develop and strengthen writing as needed by planning, revising, [and] editing" (18), with expectations for revision and independence increasing with age. Anchor Standard 10 calls for students to "write routinely over extended time frames (time for research, reflection, and revision) and shorter time frames (a single sitting or a day or two)" (18). These are not low expectations!

To be sure your students meet these ambitious standards, we encourage you to devote some time to assessing your students' on-demand writing. We recommend students engage in on-demand writing at the start and end of each unit, and that you and your students track their progress against a progression that details expectations.

Efficiency and fluency also matter. These skills come with writing often, which the standards call for students to do. "Write routinely" means to make writing a habit. Even noted writers describe how they have to push themselves to ensure that they write every day. Novelist Margaret Atwood, who has published dozens of fiction and nonfiction books and has received almost every known award for her writing, claims, "The fact is the blank pages inspire me with terror. What will I put on them? Will it be good enough? Will I have to throw it out? The trick is to sit at the desk anyway, every day" (Donald Murray, *Shoptalk: Learning to Write with Writers*, 1990, 72). It is not surprising that the standards emphasize writing often. Writing is just like any other practice—playing piano, running, knitting. The more opportunity you have for practice, the better you get. In these units, a day does not go by that your students are not writing. Across a week, they will write many pages. Inevitably, they will get better, faster, more fluent, more efficient, and more powerful.

A writing routine does not just come with sitting down to write, however. A writing routine involves understanding what it means to work at your writing. Writing anchor Standard 5 states that writers will "develop and strengthen writing as needed by planning, revising, editing, rewriting, or trying a new approach" (18). The CCSS are closely aligned, then, with the practices researched by Pulitzer prize–winning journalist Don Murray, documented in *A Writer Teaches*

Writing (2003). Murray described how journalists learn, even when writing to deadline, to revise on the run, to try out different leads and endings, and to consider and reconsider each word, comma, and sentence structure to convey precise meaning. In other words, they know that writing is a process.

Volume is also related to rate. Over time, students should be able to write with increasing confidence and volume. Within this curriculum, most sixth-graders will be able to produce two pages in a forty-minute sitting, and by eighth grade they will be able to write four pages, in the right circumstances. We have seen students sit down to write an on-demand piece at the end of a unit of study and regularly produce that much writing. When they know a lot about that which they are writing, their pencils will fly. When they are used to writing often, their fingers and minds will be ready. That level of production comes with practice.

This has led teachers to look closely at their schedules for writing, following a student across a week, seeing how much time is actually available for that student to write, and paying attention to how much writing he or she produces during one sitting. In every school where kids become powerful writers, they have extended time to write, and they write daily. Don Graves, pioneer reformer in writing instruction for students, often said that if writers couldn't return to a piece of writing at least three times a week, it wasn't worth doing at all. The kids would just be too far away from their writing to remain committed to it (Graves, *Writing: Teachers and Students at Work*, 2003).

If you've ever practiced piano scales, you know that after a long stretch away from the piano, when you first sit down your fingers are slow. It's the same if you haven't exercised in a while or if you haven't picked up knitting needles in five years. You know the skills, but your legs or fingers don't respond with the speed they once did. On the other hand, as you begin to knit or run or play piano or write, you'll find that for every day you do it, the sheer discipline of moving your pen across the page or your fingers across the keyboard, you will become faster and more fluent.

THE STANDARDS CALL FOR NEW LEVELS OF PROFICIENCY

While the CCSS are notable for requiring an equal division of time between three kinds of writing and for frequent opportunities to engage in the writing process, the most remarkable thing about the CCSS is the call for high levels of proficiency. The expectations are not high for the younger grades, but they escalate between grades 5 and 8. By grade 8, a narrative writer should "Engage and orient the reader by establishing a context and point of view and introducing a narrator and/or characters" (CCSS.ELA-Literacy.W.8.3a). So the writer is supposed to establish a context and point of view, something that middle schoolers often have trouble comprehending in their reading lives, and introduce a narrator and other characters. And all of that just describes one aspect of narrative writing! Many teachers no doubt think, "Could I write like that, with that much power and concision, let alone teach a thirteen-year-old to write like that?" The expectations are especially high when one looks at some of the middle school sample texts included in Appendix C.

If you go to Appendix C in the CCSS, page 42 (see http://www.corestandards.org/assets/Appendix_C.pdf, Google search terms "CCSS Appendix C"), you will see an example of the kind of writing seventh-graders should be able to do as information writers. It begins like this:

A Geographical Report

My report is on a very rare and unique wetland that many people do not even know exists. They occur only in a few places around the world.

My topic is created by a specific geographical condition. Vernal pools in San Diego occur only on the local mesas and terraces, where soil conditions allow, but these are the ideal place for much of the city's urban and agricultural development. Is it possible to find a balance between the two conflicting purposes of expansion and preservation?

This raises an interesting question; how can you establish vernal pools being thought of as a geographical asset?

METHODS

To answer my question I had to get information on vernal pools: what they are, where they are, and how they are a sensitive natural habitat. Then I needed to examine how city expansion is affecting vernal pools, and if it is apt to continue. I needed to know what the City thinks about the problem and what they are planning to do.

First I looked for any information available on vernal pools at public libraries, but I couldn't find what I was looking for. The topic is apparently too obscure. Next I went to a university library that had an environmental department to get as much information as possible (University of San Diego).

The pieces in the appendix are not all of even quality. Sometimes one type of writing at a grade level will represent what we might think are relatively low standards, while another piece, like this one, seems high. You'll need to look between the descriptors, the grade-level specifics in the standards, and the pieces themselves to try to build a coherent vision of proficiency levels if you're interested in doing this work. By the end of the year, you should be able to create your own Appendix C, with student exemplars from your community and curriculum.

Chapter 3

The Essentials of Writing Instruction

W HENEVER I work with educators in a school, school district, city, or county, I make a point of trying to learn about the vision guiding the approach to teaching writing. I ask, "What is the Bill of Rights that guides your work with your students as writers?" When people look quizzical, I rephrase my question. "Think of it this way—when a student enters your school, what is the promise that you make to the student and her parents about the writing education that she will receive?"

Chances are good that in math, the school essentially promises that young person, "Whether your teacher likes math or not, you'll be taught math every day. You won't need to *luck out* to get a teacher who teaches math. And the course of study that you receive from one teacher won't be all that different from what your friend will receive from another teacher." Schools should make that same promise to students about writing.

"When a student enters your school, what promise do you make about the writing education he or she will receive."

The first step a district or school needs to make toward developing a standards-based approach to writing is to decide that the whole school needs to be in on this work together. Writing, like reading and math, is one of those subjects that affect a learner's ability to succeed in other subjects. So the promise a school makes to students as writers shouldn't be that different from the promise the school makes to students as mathematicians or as readers. Across a school, there needs to be a shared commitment to teach writing, and some infrastructure that assures enough of a curriculum that teachers can stand on the shoulders of prior instruction. In this chapter, I share the essentials—the *bottom-line conditions*, as we've come to call them—that school systems that provide effective writing instruction offer students.

Writing needs to be taught like any other basic skill, with explicit instruction and ample opportunity for practice. Writing is equally as complicated and as important as reading, so it makes sense to start by assuming that language arts time is equally divided between instruction in writing and reading.

Sometimes teachers will say, "I don't really teach writing per se, we do writing across the curriculum." As important as it is for students to write across the curriculum doing so doesn't take the place of a coherent, deliberate writing curriculum. Using math and reading across the curriculum are also important, yet no one suggests that the fact that math is used during a science lab means that therefore it is not also important to explicitly teach math. Assigning students to jot notes as they watch a film about colonial America or to trace the characters' development in their novel doesn't substitute for a sequential, coherent writing curriculum.

When a teacher describes her writing instruction by saying, "We just weave writing across the curriculum," she is probably saying, "I don't explicitly teach writing." But the problem is that writers, like mathematicians, need sequential, explicit instruction. Like reading and math, writing is a skill that develops over time. Students deserve writing to be a subject that is taught and studied, and this requires allotting time (that most precious resource of all) to the cause.

Furthermore, during writing time, students need to actually write. Just as learners become skilled at playing an instrument or swimming or reading by actually doing those things, writing too is learned through practice. Just as my sons' tennis teacher says, "Success in tennis has everything to do with the number of balls hit," so, too, success in reading directly correlates with the number of hours spent reading. John Guthrie's study ("Teaching for Literacy Engagement," in *Journal of Literacy Research*, 2004) illustrates that fourth-graders who read at the second-grade level spend a half-hour a day reading, while fourth-graders who read at the eighth-grade level spend four and a half hours a day reading. Success in writing, like success in reading or tennis or swimming, is directly related to the amount of time a person spends doing that thing. This means that day after day, students need to write. They need to write for long stretches of time—for something like forty minutes during writing instruction and ideally more time across the day and during homework.

Writing, like reading and math, is a skill that develops over time. Because of this, more and more schools are recognizing that students deserve writing to be a subject that is taught and studied just like reading or math. In many middle schools, writing is taught as a subject, similarly to reading. In other schools, language arts is equally divided between reading and writing, with writing being taught approximately every other month (and relied upon during alternate months).

And this means that students will have evidence to show that demonstrates their volume of writing. Accumulating this evidence probably matters, because if no one notices the volume of writing that students do, it's all too easy for students to end up writing very little. Because writing stays in a student's notebook or folder at least until the work culminates with publication, a teacher, coach, or principal can easily look through a student's collection of recent work and see the volume of work the student has produced on Monday, Tuesday, Wednesday, and so forth.

Of course, it is not only the evidence of a volume of writing that matters; evidence of growth also matters. How has the writing changed since a month

> *"A wonderful thing about writing is that it's immediately visible. This allows a school system to hold itself accountable for ensuring that every student has the opportunity and the responsibility to write every day."*

ago? The answer to this question is immediately evident when students keep their writing in a notebook, folder, or portfolio.

Writers write. A wonderful thing about writing is that it's immediately visible. This allows a school system to hold itself accountable for ensuring that every student has the opportunity and the responsibility to write every day.

Students deserve to write for real, to write the kinds of texts that they see in the world, and to write for an audience of readers, not just for the teacher's red pen.

Donald Murray, the Pulitzer prize–winning writer who is widely regarded as the father of the writing process, recalls the piano lessons he was given as a student. The school system announced that anyone wanting to learn to play the piano should report to the cafeteria after school. Murray recalls his palpable excitement: at last, he was going to learn to make those beautiful melodies! In the cafeteria, students sat in rows, facing the front. Each student was given a cardboard keyboard and shown how to lay his or her hands on it so as to "play" notes. Students pressed their cardboard keyboards, but there was no music, no melody. Murray left and never returned.

Young people deserve opportunities to write real writing; this means that instead of writing merely "pieces," "tasks," and "assignments," students need to write in all the genres that exist in the world. A student should know that he or she is writing *something*—a nonfiction book, a book review, an editorial, a lab report, a fantasy story—that writers write and readers read. The types of writing that are highlighted in the CCSS—opinion, information, and narrative writing—need to be regarded as umbrellas, with more specific genres under each umbrella. *Argument writing* is not the term most writers use—they are more apt to say they are writing an editorial, an op-ed column, a blog, or a persuasive letter, and those are the kinds of writing that students need to tackle. The student needs to know, too, that others have written this same kind of thing and that one of the best ways to learn is to study the work others have made, asking, "What did he do that I could try in my writing?"

Youngsters not only deserve daily opportunities to write particular kinds of things—to write something that exists in the world—they also deserve

opportunities to write for someone—for readers who will respond to what they have written. They deserve to write knowing that their writing stands a good chance of being read by readers. Otherwise how will young writers learn that writing well involves aiming to create an effect? Craft and deliberate choice in writing are the result of thinking, as one writes, "They'll laugh at this part," "This will build tension and suspense," or "This will make them want to know all about it." To write with this sense of agency, students need to see readers respond to their writing. They need to share their writing with partners, to read it aloud to small groups, and to have people respond as readers do—laughing at the funny parts, gasping at the sad parts, leaning forward to learn more.

Giving students opportunities to write *something* (a letter, a speech) for *someone* (a younger class, the newspaper) makes it likely that writing will engage the students and they will feel what they are doing is real, credible, and substantial. Young people should not be asked to learn to play music on cardboard keyboards or to learn to write on photocopied work sheets.

Writers write to put meaning onto the page. Students deserve the opportunity to invest themselves in their writing by choosing to write about subjects that are important to them.

Try this. Pick up a pen and write a few sentences about the sequence of actions you did today before picking up this book.

Now pause and try something different. Think about a moment in your life that for some reason really affected you. It might be the tiniest of moments, but it gave you a lump in your throat; it made your heart skip. The last time you saw someone. The time you realized you could actually do that thing you'd been longing to do. Write (or think through) the story of that indelible moment. On the page (or just in your mind's eye), try to capture the essence of that bit of life.

Try one more. Think of a subject on which you are an expert. If you were to teach a class on a topic, what would it be? What if that course was done through writing—how would you start the first lesson?

You will find that picking up your pen and writing a few sentences about the sequence of actions you just did—a kind of writing in which you throw out any old words—is absolutely unlike the other kind of writing in which you reach for the precise words that capture something important to you. For students to learn to write and grow as writers, it is essential that they are invested in their writing and that they care about writing well. Students (indeed, all of us) are far more apt to be invested if they are writing about subjects they know and care about and if they are writing for real, responsive readers.

It is hard to imagine an argument *against* letting students choose their own topics for most of the writing they do in the writing workshop. Of course when students are writing as part of a study of *To Kill a Mockingbird* or World War II or black holes, you will channel them to write about a specific subtopic related to the cross-disciplinary unit. But during the time in the day when students are working specifically on their writing skills, they'll work their hardest if they can choose their own subjects. Although the craft, strategies, qualities of good writing, and the processes of writing vary depending on whether someone is writing an editorial or an information book, good writing does not vary based on whether the information book is teaching about kinds of jazz or the special demands placed on a lacrosse goalie. Teachers can gather the entire class together and teach them a lesson in a particular genre—for example, the importance of detail or elaboration—knowing the instruction will be equally relevant to students who are engaged in writing on any one of an array of subjects.

When students have the opportunity and responsibility to choose their own subjects, they are not only much more apt to be invested in their writing, but they are also likely to know more about a topic of choice, and writing well requires information and insight on the topic. Of course, writing also requires deeper learning, which means that students will progress from writing about what they know to writing to grow new ideas.

Students deserve to be explicitly taught how to write. Instruction matters—and this includes instruction in spelling and conventions, as well as in the qualities and strategies of good writing.

It is not enough to simply turn down the lights, turn on the music, and say to students, "Write." Nor is it okay to take anything that they produce and say, "You are an author!" It is not enough for students to be assigned to do this or that writing task. We wouldn't dream of simply turning down the lights, turning up the music, and saying, "Do math," and then later collecting the students' work and proclaiming, "You are all mathematicians!" Nor would we dream of simply assigning and collecting a math task in lieu of teaching math. Yet it's common for teachers to think that assigning writing can substitute for teaching. It doesn't.

Writers need instruction. Writing improves in a palpable, dramatic fashion when students are given explicit instruction, lots of time to write, clear goals, and powerful feedback.

For example, if a student is writing an information book about diabetes, the student is not going to discover on her own how to choose a logical order—do her subsections proceed chronologically from signs that one has diabetes through diagnosis and onto treatment, or does the text overview kinds of diabetes and discuss each kind in order of severity, from the mildest to the most severe? It's not in students' DNA to naturally evolve as writers that use structure to highlight their meaning. Instead, that needs to be taught.

I can walk into a classroom, look over students' writing, and know immediately whether students are being taught to write because strong, clear instruction dramatically and visibly affects student writing. When teachers explicitly teach the qualities, habits, and strategies of effective writing, that writing becomes better—and the improvement is evident within days and weeks, not just months. Writing is one of very few areas in which a teacher can make a covenant with students saying, "I'm going to teach you something and if you work hard your writing will improve in dramatic ways within just three to four weeks."

One of the powerful things about writing instruction is that a good deal of it is multileveled. Say a writer is writing an information text about weather. If that writer has piled all that he or she knows onto a random assortment of sections, chances are good that it will make an enormous difference to suggest the writer think carefully about what the sections of his text should be and how to arrange them. A student who labors to write a few pages a day and a student who easily writes reams can benefit equally from that instruction. Both students, too, can look at a published information book to notice what the author has done that he or she could emulate. Actually, most strategies and qualities of good writing are multileveled. Some students will spell better than others, and some will use more complex sentence structures than others, but many of the skills and strategies of skilled writing are within reach of every writer.

Students deserve the opportunity and instruction necessary for them to cycle through the writing process as they write: rehearsing, drafting, revising, editing, and publishing their writing.

The scientific method is widely regarded as so fundamental to science that students use it whether they are studying sinking and floating in kindergarten or friction and inertia in high school. In a similar way, the writing process is fundamental to all writing; therefore, it is important that students of every age receive frequent opportunities to rehearse, draft, revise, and edit their writing.

The important thing to realize is that teaching students the process of writing is not the same as teaching them the names of presidents. The point is not for them to be able to parrot back the steps of writing well. The reason it is important for students to know the writing process is that when they aspire to write something, knowing the process is like knowing the recipe. For example, if a student is going to write an information article about presidential elections, her first concern should probably not be "What is my first sentence?' Instead, she'd do well to think first, "How does an article like this tend to go?" and "What kinds of structures could be good to use to organize this text?"

Of course, becoming at home with the process of writing is not unlike becoming at home with the process of doing long division or of solving word problems. It takes repeated practice. One learns and becomes more efficient over time. Things that once took a long time become quicker, more internalized, and more automatic.

This means that most of the time, it is useful for students to have opportunities to plan for and rehearse writing, to flash-draft, and to reread their rough draft, thinking, "How can I make this even better?" Feedback from a reader can help a writer imagine ways to improve the draft. A writer should always write with the conventions that are easily under his control, but once a text is almost ready for readers, the writer will want to edit it, taking extra care to make the text clearer and more correct. Often the writer will use outside assistance—from a partner or teacher—to edit.

Students deserve opportunities to read and to hear texts read, and to read as insiders, studying what other authors have done that they too could try.

Any effective writing curriculum acknowledges the importance of writers being immersed in powerful writing. Students learn to write from being engrossed in and affected by texts other authors have written. They need the sounds and power of good literature and strong nonfiction texts to seep into their bones. They need a sense of how an effective bit of persuasion can sway readers, for the way a poem can make a reader gasp and be still.

Students especially need opportunities to read as writers. Imagine that you were asked to write a foreword for this book. My hunch is that you'd likely do what I did when Georgia Heard asked me to write my first foreword ever. I pulled books from my shelf and searched for forewords. I found half a dozen and read them ravenously. "How does a foreword really go?" I asked.

By studying the work of other authors, writers learn the conventions of particular kinds of text. Writers tuck cautionary advice into a series of steps. Storytellers reference the weather to convey the passage of time or to amplify the mood. By studying texts that resemble those they are trying to write, students learn the tools of their trade. The Common Core places a high priority on students learning to read like writers. Thinking about the reasons why an author may have chosen specific language (RL.4), structures (RL.5), or perspectives (RL.6), students learn to be attuned to the deliberate decisions an author seems to have made by making their own similar decisions as they write and revise in hopes of creating particular effects.

Students deserve clear goals and frequent feedback. They need to hear ways their writing is getting better and to know what their next steps might be.

Research by John Hattie (*Visible Learning for Teachers*, 2012) and others has shown that to support learners' progress, it is important for them to work toward crystal clear goals and to receive feedback that shows them both what they are doing well and what their next steps are apt to be. Learners across a wide range of fields—people training to be Olympic divers, world-class chess players, or competitive figure skaters—know that it is not practice alone that makes for perfection, it is deliberate, goal-driven practice.

The bottom-line conditions for effective writing instruction are, then:

- Writing needs to be taught like any other basic skill, with explicit instruction and ample opportunity for practice.

- Aspiring writers deserve to write for real purposes, to write the kinds of texts that they see in the world, and to write for an audience of readers.

- Writers write to put meaning onto the page. Adolescents will invest themselves in their writing when they choose subjects and topics that are important to them.

- Young people deserve to be explicitly taught how to write, both the skills and strategies of writers as well as the conventions.

- Students deserve the opportunity and instruction to cycle through the writing process.

- To write well, adolescents need opportunities to read and to hear texts read, and to read as writers.

- Learners need clear goals and frequent feedback.

Middle School Writers and the Writing Process

W HEN I WAS AN EIGHTH-GRADER, my teacher taught writing by assigning us topics and telling us the expected page length. We wrote at home, bringing our completed essays, book reports, and summaries to school a few days after they were assigned. After a bit, we received the papers back, each with a grade and some red marks in the margins that noted grammatical mistakes. I expect many of us were "taught" writing that way. That was before the Writing Revolution.

A THUMBNAIL HISTORY OF WRITING PROCESS INSTRUCTION

Approximately three decades ago, a flurry of books and articles called for a writing revolution. Peter Elbow, Donald Murray, James Moffett, Ken Macrorie, and a series of edited volumes titled *Writers at Work* combined to popularize the message that when writers write, they do not sit down with a quill pen and immediately produce graceful, compelling prose. Instead, writers work through *a process of writing*, a process that contains recursive stages.

The Common Core State Standards reinforce the message that writing instruction must involve teaching students this process of writing. The Anchor Standards for Writing name the process as "planning, revising, editing, rewriting" (CCSS.ELA-Literacy. CCRA.W.5). Perhaps because so many writers have made public how they write, there is no dispute about writing process. Whether you are a journalist or a novelist, a blogger or a writer of textbooks, whether you go through these stages in forty minutes or over five years, writers take their writing through stages of planning, revising, and getting ready to publish.

Different people use different terms when describing those stages. For example, what the CCSS calls planning, some call *prewriting* and others *rehearsal*, but either way, widespread agreement has emerged that writers spend time preparing for writing. This stage involves living like a researcher—collecting material for writing, weighing alternative plans for how a piece of writing might go, talking about one's topic, reading texts that resemble the text one hopes to write, and doing the research one needs to write with authority.

Writers also *draft*. Early drafts are more like playing in clay than inscribing in marble; a writer might try alternative leads, explore different voices for a text, or freewrite, keeping her eyes glued on the subject and trying to capture the contours of it in tentative form. Writers shift back and forth between drafting and revising.

Revision means, quite literally, "to see again." During revision, a writer pulls back from a draft to reread and rethink, "What is it I really want to say? What structure might best bring readers along to (and through) my content?" Writers revise to convey meaning and to make that meaning clear and potent to readers. Revision may involve rewriting an introduction, reconsidering one's evidence, and elaborating on important sections while deleting unimportant ones. Revision usually involves anticipating a reader's response. A writer may ask, "What do I want my readers to think early on when they begin reading? Later? What do I want them to feel and do in response?" Revision usually involves at least a second and often a third draft, since revisions that are bound by the contours of a first draft are held to the original structure, pace, and voice.

Finally, writers *edit*, which involves smoothing out, linking, tightening, clarifying, fact checking, and correcting. During editing, writers think about spelling, punctuation, and word choice, yes, but writers also think about precise details, language, and clarity.

All of that sounds like a very long and arduous process, but there are times when a text is written quickly—say, in an hour or in half an hour. Even when writing quickly, writers still tend to go through abbreviated versions of each of these steps of the writing process.

Research on the writing process initially influenced especially college-level courses. Don Murray's journalism courses at the University of New Hampshire became models for courses taught at many other colleges. Graduate freshman comp courses sprang up everywhere, and everywhere they were informed by research on writing process. Meanwhile, professional journalists began studying the writing process: Chip Scanlon and Roy Peter Clark taught journalists at Poynter Institute, and Murray at the Boston Globe. Soon, of course, these courses were being taught also in high schools.

Then three decades ago, a team of us from the University of New Hampshire—Donald Graves, Susan Sowers, and I, broke the news that even young kids could experience the writing process. The National Institute of Education study that we conducted helped the world realize that when teachers invite school-age writers to write like the pros write and then observe and coach them in their process of writing as well as responding to their products, their growth in writing could be spectacular. The research on young people and the writing process was the talk of the town back in the eighties.

Since then, the idea that educators need to teach the writing process has become so accepted that it's a mainstream premise. Many standardized tests even include planning pages, and remind writers to leave time to plan, revise, and edit their essays. Most language arts textbooks have incorporated the terms (if not the true concepts) of the writing process into their curriculum. And the Common Core State Standards leave no doubt that all students are expected to develop facility in the process of writing. It's anchor standard 5 for writing that reads, in full: "Develop and strengthen writing as needed by planning, revising, editing, rewriting, or trying a new approach" (CCSS.ELA-Literacy.CCRA.W.5), and it's anchor standard 10 for writing that reads, "Write routinely over extended time frames (time for research, reflection, and revision) and shorter time frames (a single sitting or a day or two) for a range of tasks, purposes, and audiences" (CCSS.ELA-Literacy.CCRA.W.10). More than this, the written products included in the appendix as benchmarks for student writing signal to any knowledgeable teacher that for students to meet the ambitious standards of the Common Core, they need to be explicitly taught the skills, strategies, and qualities of good writing—and the Common Core Standards themselves were taken through draft after draft.

AN OVERVIEW OF INSTRUCTIONAL APPROACHES TO THE WRITING PROCESS

Although the rhetoric behind the idea of teaching the writing process involves talk like this—"Students should be invited to write like real writers"—the truth is that a thirteen-year-old will not write exactly like Thomas Friedman, Robert Frost, or Malcolm Gladwell, nor would all adult writers be able to do that! Teachers who adopt a writing process approach to teaching writing still must think through what the writing process will be that they plan to teach their students and how they will go about teaching that process.

I see teachers often choosing one of these three possible approaches to teaching writing process:

- The "free to be me" approach
- The "assigned task" approach
- The "demonstrate, scaffold, release to write" approach

Here, I'll outline the assumptions underlying each of these approaches, before moving on to a detailed look at our approach, teaching units of study in a writing workshop, which is modeled on the third approach.

The Free to Be Me Approach

Following the free to be me approach, some teachers encourage each young person to find his or her own individual writing process and project. On any one day in these classrooms, one writer will write introductions to an information book, another will write a fiction story, and yet another will write several poems. In these classrooms, students cycle through the writing process in their own way and at their own pace. In a month, one student in a class may have written one very long rough draft, another will have worked three pieces through a series of revisions, and still another will have produced a dozen lightly revised texts. Teachers in these classrooms also place a priority on each writer choosing his or her genre and topic. The teachers, meanwhile, look for teachable moments in which they can extend what students do as writers.

The explicit belief that teachers express when arguing for this approach is that engagement is everything and that the primary concern is simply to get students writing in the first place. You often see this approach in alternative settings. There are at least two problems, though, with this approach. First, it takes a mythic teacher to actually follow each writer along through different genres and different parts of the process, helping each writer find mentor texts, and teaching each writer strategies specific to that genre and that stage of the writing process. Often, even with the best of intentions,

"I believe that all writers benefit from strategies to help them get started, take their writing through stages of revision, and see their writing improve as a result of expert instruction."

these writers are left to do their best, with some cheering from the sidelines. Secondly, therefore, an implicit, underlying belief system of this approach is that the ability to write is natural to all of us, within our DNA, and that under the right conditions, kids will come to writing on their own, needing "invitations" more than explicit instruction. This is neither my belief, nor am I a proponent of this approach, not because I don't believe engagement matters—it does—but because I believe that all writers benefit from strategies to help them get started and take their writing through stages of revision, and all writers become engaged as they see their writing improve as the result of expert instruction.

The Assigned Tasks Approach

At the opposite extreme, there are teachers who teach writing by assigning writing. Often in these classrooms, the writing curriculum is a series of tasks that are replicas of (or sometimes interim steps toward) the task students will see on high-stakes assessments. It is not unusual for the students to be prompted to write about a text the teacher has selected and the whole class has studied together, and often the teacher will have helped the class gather some of the ideas and information that will later become the content of the work students produce in response to assigned tasks. Each student, then, is assigned to write a paper of the same format, about the same text, using the same ideas the class has developed together.

The tasks may be sequenced so that later tasks are more challenging than earlier tasks, so that the work of each step can be assembled into a larger project. For example, students might first be told to "write a paragraph describing character A, from text number 1. Be sure to give evidence by drawing on three examples from the text." Next, students might be assigned to do the same for text number 2. Finally, the student is told to "write an essay comparing and contrasting character A from text number 1 with character B from text number 2. Be sure you address at least three similarities and three differences and make references to both texts."

Rather than teaching replicable *ways* writers plan, structure, sequence, or revise their writing, teachers specify each specific step students are to take, waiting until everyone has completed that step before progressing on. Alternately, teachers may give students graphic organizers that they fill out as part of each step. The tasks might be laid out step by step in a stop-and-go process such as: (1) Show your planning work using this graphic organizer. (2) Write a thesis and three supporting topic sentences on this graphic organizer. List the evidence you will include under each topic sentence. (3) Write a three-part essay, following your outline. Your work should be written in complete sentences with correct punctuation.

The assumption is that assigning the writing process is a sufficient enough way to teach it. If there is feedback given, it usually involves an assessment as to whether students fulfilled expectations. The feedback is task-specific and not designed to transfer to other pieces of writing. Again, as is probably clear, this approach is not one I endorse, because it gives the illusion that kids have become independent writers, but really they have become obedient writers. Often they are not flexible, resourceful, or resilient enough to write for a variety of tasks, and often they struggle when writing becomes hard, because they have a false sense of competency.

The Demonstrate, Scaffold, Release to Write Approach

My colleagues and I fall into a third category—as do many others who care about the teaching of the writing process. Our goal is to actively and explicitly teach students to draw on a repertoire of skills and strategies that have served accomplished writers well over the years. We look for evidence that students have the knowledge, skills, and habits to draw on these planning, drafting, revising, and editing skills whether they are working on extended writing projects or on a flash-draft. To help students develop the repertoire of skills for each stage of the writing process, we *demonstrate* the process that writers often use to do the type of writing being studied, and we *scaffold* students to practice the steps of the process, so that when we *release* them to write without support, they are able to independently draw on the repertoire of strategies we've taught. As students continue to write with less scaffolding, we teach by using assessments and goals, feedback, and guided practice.

A RATIONALE FOR CHOOSING THE THIRD APPROACH AND A DESCRIPTION OF HOW THIS TRANSLATES INTO UNITS OF STUDY FOR A WRITING WORKSHOP

To understand what this third approach—our approach—to teaching writing involves, consider this metaphor. Think, for a moment, about the way a ski instructor travels down a mountain with a class of students. We argue that when students travel roughly in sync through steps in the writing process, it provides extra teaching opportunities that are not unlike the sort a ski instructor finds at intervals down the mountain. If the instructor says, "See those hay bales alongside that pole? Let's stop there. Before you get to those bales, these are the techniques that will help you . . ." Then the young skiers receive some demonstration teaching and lots of pointers. After skiing to the interim spot of the hay bales, there is time for assessment and another "See that rise, where that cluster of skiers have stopped to look at the view? Let's stop there. This time, let's work on something I'll show you right now . . ." This sort of instruction allows a teacher to do a lot of explicit teaching. Often the instructor intersperses interludes for this kind of explicit instruction with times when kids zoom down the hill, putting into play the moves they have learned, practicing and polishing them.

As long as the process you teach rings true—that is, it is a process that real writers, and learners of any type, might actually participate in—and as long as students are invested in their writing and you are teaching strategies that help them write well beyond this piece, this sort of synchronized progression through the writing process seems to us to be warranted.

So now let's imagine that we want to teach argument writing to seventh-graders. We'd want students to be working in sync with one another for the first part of the unit so that we can teach them strategies they'll find helpful, so we'd need to decide on a sequence of shared tasks. Perhaps we'd first pose a need for students to write persuasive letters on an authentic, disputed topic in which they are stakeholders. We'd then ask students to engage in quick research around the disputed issue, teaching them how argument writers weigh and evaluate evidence to develop a position. Then we'd engage them in a longer effort to write research-based argument essays on disputed issues of their own choosing. The unit would involve a sequence of tasks, not assignment-based but instead writing process-based, and therefore transferable to kids' work beyond the task at hand.

Through this, students would develop and then draw upon a growing repertoire of strategies for each step of the argument-writing process. For example, at the beginning of the research process, we'd teach students strategies for suspending judgment and of not only weighing and evaluating evidence, but evaluating sources as well. We'd teach them to consider their specific audience, and to tailor their argument for that audience. We'd teach them to use debate practices to anticipate the counterargument, addressing it in their draft. We'd teach them to keep an eye on deadlines, and to use planning to remind themselves of all that they know how to do. The goal, therefore, is not only to support students in drafting one piece of argument writing—instead, the goal is for students to develop and draw upon a repertoire of strategies that will last their whole lives so they emerge from this unit of study as writers who could tackle any argument task—speeches, position papers, editorials—with confidence.

In life, one will not always have an instructor at one's side, setting goals, assessing, and planning. So it is also important for instruction to happen in gradually less frequent intervals that are designed to give learners time to assume some of the instructor's role. The instructor might say, "This time, will you and a partner ski together and stop at the same places where we stopped, only this time, will the two of you watch each other and give each other some feedback?" Then again, the instructor might say, "This lesson is about to end, but why don't you take a few more runs? Let's review the things you need to work on. And listen—make the first run on a blue beginner trail, and only move up to the advanced black diamond one if you feel confident on that first trail." It is in just that way that teachers of writing teach—working with a sequence of tasks, and explicitly teaching strategies and skills but also removing scaffolds as quickly as possible to give students longer chunks of time within which to do their *own* work.

It is important to point out that writers need to be able to plan, draft, revise, and edit while producing work for fast-approaching deadlines, so the process that I've just described can also be accelerated, with rehearsal occurring in the mind's eye, with revision happening during rehearsal. Instruction needs to support both the more extended and the more abbreviated writing processes so that students learn that these are variations of each other. That is, even when a writer must produce a text within an hour, the proficient writer can still call on an intense, if abbreviated, version of the writing process.

As a unit of study unrolls (and also as the year unrolls and as one year follows the next), students work on more challenging tasks and with more independence. Perhaps after students have progressed in sync through one or two cycles of opinion writing, doing the work we described to produce persuasive letters and editorials, the teacher might alert the class to a real issue that has arisen in the community and suggest that students choose the form of persuasive writing they most want to use to address that issue, angling their writing to the audience they want to address, and writing quickly—perhaps over the space of just two days—transferring all they have learned previously to their effort to address a timely issue in their community.

In the demonstrate, scaffold, release approach, how does one calibrate the challenge level of instruction?

Of course, as the ski instruction continues, the student progresses from blue trails to black diamond trails. In the same way, the writing work that students tackle becomes progressively more challenging.

For example, toward the start of a sixth-grade school year, when working with students who are new to the writing process, you might teach a unit in which students write information texts on topics of personal expertise. Within that unit, you will presumably teach your students to think about the logical structure of their topic and to use the table of contents as a way to structure the draft. Two months later, you or a colleague who teaches social studies or science might begin yet another information writing unit, this one on writing research reports. When coaching students to progress through the writing process on their research reports, you will remind them of strategies they used earlier when writing information texts on topics of personal expertise. "Do you remember how you thought about the component parts of your topic and made a table of contents? Well, you will want to do that again for this new topic, but this time you need to check your sources to be sure that the subtopics you imagine addressing are ones on which you can find adequate information." Students will probably still be encouraged to work with the structure of their texts in very concrete ways by drafting and revising their tables of contents, but you may keep in mind that your very strongest students could be graduated from that reliance on a table of contents. It is far more challenging to use transitions not only within a section of a text but also between those sections. When writers forego a table of contents and try to stitch together the chunks of an extended piece of writing, they often need help learning about A heads, B heads, and C heads and certainly need to learn to use a hierarchy of transition phrases within an extended text. My point is, however, that teaching writing involves rallying students to tackle a progression of writing challenges. In middle school, that means planning curriculum so that students have opportunities for repeated practice. It also means planning across the curriculum, so that students are doing meaningful nonfiction writing in social studies and science.

THE DISTINCTIVE CHARACTERISTICS OF MIDDLE SCHOOL STUDENTS' WRITING PROCESS

Of course, concomitant with deciding on the approach you will use with your students and with thinking through the ways this approach will allow you to differentiate your teaching based on your particular students' needs, you also need to consider the age of your students and the volume and pace of work you can expect of them, as well as what materials—paper, iPads, or laptops—will be needed for them to be successful. As I outline next, these expectations vary across the grades, and you'll want to be sure you not only provide the writing tools to set your students up for success, but that you also set high—but achievable—goals for the amount of writing your students do in a day, a week, a month, and for the speed at which they will move through the writing process.

Stamina and Pacing across the Grades

As students become older and more experienced, they are able to write with more fluency and more quickly. By the time a student is in eighth grade, the student should be able to produce a quick and competent flash-draft—perhaps two and a half or three pages in length—within forty-five minutes. If pressed to do so, this student can speed through the process of deliberation over the focus and structure of a text to simply pick up the pen and write. For such a student, writing a flash-draft is a familiar process because he or she has done this so many times.

It is perhaps more significant to say, however, that by the time a student is in eighth grade, he or she can plan strategically for work on a piece of writing that will span several weeks. Such a writer will plan not only the content but

will also plan by anticipating challenges he or she will need to meet and the strategies that will be needed. Such a writer could seek out mentor texts, and ask to see a rubric or checklist, or make one for him- or herself if one were not available. Such a writer could work productively on a single piece of writing over a sequence of weeks, shifting from planning to drafting, to assessing and revising, and then, to planning and drafting again.

That is, an eighth-grader who has grown up in a writing workshop has enough rehearsal and revision strategies in his or her repertoire, and enough ability and skill at self-assessment and knowledge of good writing, that the student can, with coaching and feedback, sustain work on a piece of writing for a long stretch of time, and that time would be worth it.

One of the important things to realize when thinking about how writing processes develop over time is that a more pressing deadline and briefer writing process can sometimes mean that the challenge level of the task has increased, but it is more apt to mean that the challenge level has *decreased*, requiring the writer to do less deliberate, strategic thinking. Producing an entire piece of writing within a more focused span of time can lower the challenge level of the work if this leads a writer to forgo deliberation and strategic work.

When thinking about how the writing process of a sixth-grader differs from that of a eighth-grader, then, the first thing to note is that many middle schools find that their feeder elementary schools do not send all their students up to middle school with the same experience with writing. In those instances, sixth-grade teachers (or fifth-grade teachers, whatever grade is the first grade in middle school), often find that they need to do some recapitulation of curriculum. If you teach in middle schools where your elementary schools are also teaching writing workshop, it is critical for sixth-grade teachers to visit some of the fifth-grade classrooms (or at least to study on-demand and published pieces from fifth-grade) in the spring, to research what kids already know. Avoid recapitulating curriculum for sixth-graders who know a lot about writing.

Students who are new to middle school are also somewhat thrown by the shift from spending most of the day with a single teacher who knew them well and was responsible for their academic and social well-being, to moving from room to room, teacher to teacher, not knowing if there is any single adult who is watching over them. Meanwhile, your new middle school students are going into puberty. All of those things are true everywhere, and they account for some of the reasons that sixth-grade writers are different than eighth-graders. Your eighth-graders are older, more mature, and they have spent three years becoming expert in writing process.

Your entering students, then, are not apt to have the capacity to sustain work on a single text for as long. They often don't have a repertoire of rehearsal and revision strategies that merits them spending weeks on a single piece, especially if that piece is three pages long. It may seem counterintuitive to suggest that younger students write more texts than older students, but bear in mind that kindergarten students write five pieces a day and, at the start of the year, first-graders tend to write a new piece every day or two. So don't think that there is something inherently advanced about writing an entire text in one day and then revising and editing it the next day! It tends to be the mark of a less mature writer, who can't sustain attention to a piece for long.

Revision across the Grades

Between sixth and eighth grade, students' abilities to revise become more sophisticated. Revision for experienced writers begins much earlier in the writing process. As should be clear from my discussion of rehearsal strategies, as your students grow up participating in writing workshops, revision will actually begin when they draft a timeline or an outline and use these plans to help them anticipate difficulties and then to imagine new possibilities for the upcoming draft. Similarly, when experienced writers draft and revise leads, they eventually do so not only with an eye toward a good lead but also with recognition that each lead represents a different way the text could go: "If I start it this way, it'll take too long to get to the main part." By eighth grade, kids begin to grasp that the process of writing a position statement is actually the process of writing an essay, in miniature.

So, if you teach sixth-graders, you will sometimes want them to ski the mountain quickly and sometimes slowly. Slow for a sixth-grader won't be as slow as what you can expect of an eighth-grader. When a sixth-grader prolongs work on a single text, taking time to vary the kinds of elaboration he or she uses, to include examples and discuss them, for example, that work will probably span a week and a half of writing workshops. On the other hand, although your eighth-graders will also sometimes write flash-drafts or cycle through the entire writing process in a few days (or even in a day), these students can also work for longer stretches of time. The biggest difference between sixth and eighth grade involves the scale of revision work, with eighth-graders often writing many drafts and often shifting between writing and then studying a mentor text or researching before resuming writing. Eighth-graders, too, are apt to work on texts that are considerably longer than those written by sixth-graders. A typical personal narrative for a sixth-grader will probably be three pages, whereas a narrative nonfiction piece by an eighth-grader, such as a piece of investigative journalism, might be five or six pages.

Writing Tools across the Grades

There is one other way that your eighth-graders will become more competent, and that is with how they work digitally. Most of your students will take the SATs online now, they will write papers in high school and college on computers, and they will become the kind of writers who not only type final pieces, but work across the writing process digitally. Most adult writers begin their writing now on a laptop, and take their writing through multiple stages of revision that way. Sometimes we are writing on shared platforms, such as Google Docs. Sometimes we are writing directly to open audiences, through blogs and other media. You want your students to be adept in these formats as well. That means that while your sixth-graders might begin pieces of writing by hand, and only sometimes "type these in" at the end, you want your eighth-graders to be efficient and competent at using the technology at hand to help them be ever more productive writers.

The notebook is a metaphor for the place where you work on your writing. For many middle school workshops, this will be a paper notebook, as that can be incredibly efficient—you don't need tech to work, there is no wait time, no one has lost their flashdrive or file. In some classrooms with reliable, available technology, the notebook might actually be a file on an iPad or laptop. What matters is that there is a place where kids are working on getting better at their writing, where they can jot notes sometimes during your lesson, where you can ask them to try something right away. Most middle school writing workshop teachers find that if students keep writer's notebooks and use those notebooks as a place to do the work involved in the stages of their writing process, then it helps the students become invested in developing processes and strategies as writers. First promulgated by Donald Murray, the Pulitzer prize–winning author of *A Writer Teaches Writing* and a score of other books on writing instruction, and journalism coach to *The Boston Globe* and the Poynter Institute, writer's notebooks have come to represent a writing process approach to teaching writing. Murray, who calls these tools *daybooks*, especially emphasizes the importance of writing often so as to "not walk around unwritten." When a person lives with a writer's notebook at his or her side, this more likely leads that person to put insights, observations, quotes, and anecdotes onto the page long before the writer has chosen a topic or begun work toward a specific writing project. Murray found that when an observation, a response to a book, an account of an experience, and some questions, for example, are laid side by side on the page, out of that mix, ideas for writing grow. "I compost my life," he says in describing "the great garage sale of junk" from which his new insights and ideas developed.

I cowrote a book in the early 1990s, *Living Between the Lines*, that especially embraces Murray's definition of writer's notebooks as the rich compost kept by a wide-awake writer. I reread that book now and feel a wave of nostalgia for an era when writing instruction in schools emphasized living the writerly life, encouraging students to pause to savor the wake of wonder left by a cicada bug. I feel enormous fondness for the image of notebooks as a "great garage sale" of entries. I hope some of the spirit of that early way of bringing the writing process into classrooms remains in this series.

You'll see us telling students that writers collect small stories in their notebooks and reread their notebooks to decide which of those stories they want to develop into major pieces of writing. You will see us suggest that writers can jot possible leads in a notebook or plan alternate structures for a text. You'll see the notebooks change as writers progress from working on narrative writing to working on essay writing. Now we'll say, "Writers don't only collect small stories. Writers also collect big ideas." During these times when we talk about the writer's notebook, there will be lots of references to our own notebooks and to the notebooks kept by published writers.

Although notebooks will predominate during rehearsal in particular, students leave those notebooks behind when they go to write draft one, which is either written on one side of lined paper, outside the notebook, so that the draft can be cut apart or can have flaps added to the margins during revision, or is on the computer. But even when students are drafting on lined paper, outside the notebook, they may return to the writer's notebook as a craftsperson returns to the workbench, to hammer out a possible ending or to refine a particular part.

But times have changed a bit, and my colleagues and I talk about writer's notebooks differently and, frankly, a bit less than we once did. We still rally students in grades 3–8 to keep writer's notebooks, and we use the presence of writer's notebooks as a physical embodiment of the writerly life. And we still talk about the importance of living with wide-awake attentiveness. Recently, we have found that one of the most important sections of a writer's notebook is a section we didn't even consider years ago, and that's the final section where writers keep track of their goals, their progress toward their goals, and their conferences.

Our emphasis on writer's notebooks has also changed because increasingly, we spend time emphasizing the role of research and the importance of structuring a text and writing within genre-specific specifications. When students are writing expository texts, where one page does not necessarily follow the next, as information needs to be sorted, chunked, and resorted, the binding of a notebook can be restrictive. If writers are researching the American Revolution and want to sort their notes to imagine perhaps writing a compare-and-contrast essay, this is not as easy to do if the notes are bound into a notebook. We are also conscious that our students are increasingly writing more and more digitally, and that that is their future. So we hold onto the notion of a notebook, but we are flexible with what that term means.

You will see, then, that in this series, we start each year with a big emphasis on writer's notebooks and on the importance of living the writerly life. We try to give continued attention to the tool of writer's notebooks throughout all the units and all the years, but the truth is that they play a less dominant role as writers work in some units that require a special amount of sorting and categorizing of information. In those units, you will see that some teachers replace notebooks with folders or digital files.

You will find other suggestions for ways materials can support the writing process, and you'll discover these suggestions as you proceed through the curriculum itself. For now, it is important to know that one of the ways to scaffold a student's writing process is to provide materials that do some of this work. It is important to know, too, that if you grew up on my earlier books and find yourself wondering, "How does the approach supported in *Units of*

Study in Argument, Information, and Narrative Writing align with the approach described in *Living Between the Lines*? (or in books such as Anne Lamott's *Bird by Bird* or Don Murray's *A Writer Teaches Writing*?)," your question is astute. As the world looks for instruction to emphasize expository writing more than narrative, structure more than detail, research more than mining personal experience, visible, accountable progress more than deeply personal investment, a sequence of tasks over an investment in authentic processes, our focus on writer's notebooks has decreased a bit, with more attention focused on writing files and booklets, portfolios, and self-assessment.

I say this to help you understand the field of writing and the history of approaches to teaching writing. I think transparency is helpful because if you understand the trail on which our thinking has taken us, you can choose to follow that trail or deviate from it. I'd be proud as punch if some of you mull over what I've written here and decide that for you, notebooks represent a more authentic, organic version of the writing process and that you'll find ways to make them more predominant in your teaching than they are in these units.

A MORE DETAILED LOOK AT THE WRITING PROCESS FOR WRITERS, GRADES 6–8

Now that you have an understanding of some of the reasons and rationales for decisions we've made in this series and have a road map for deciding on the materials you'll want to supply your students with as they write, let's look more closely at the writing process you and your students will go through—many times—in different units and genres and at various pacing.

Rehearsal for Writing

The first stage of the writing process may be called *rehearsal* or *prewriting* or *gathering entries*. Students who have grown up in writing workshops during the elementary grades will enter sixth grade able to generate ideas for writing. When asked to choose topics for writing, students who do not have a lot of writing experience, however, may sit in front of blank pages saying, "I don't have anything that I know about" or "I don't have strong opinions on anything" or "Nothing interesting happens in my life." In these instances, helping your students rehearse for writing means helping them learn strategies for generating content and learn, too, that their ideas, knowledge, and experiences *are*

worth writing about. But rehearsal is never just about generating content. It also involves planning the process and structure of a piece.

The process varies by genre and focus.

The strategies for generating ideas for writing will be somewhat different depending on whether a student is writing a literary essay, an editorial, a story, a research report, and so on. For example, when teaching students to write literary essays, I might teach them that it sometimes helps to read with a set of questions in mind: What is this text *really* about? What line or passage in this text captures what the author is mostly trying to convey? Then again, I might let them know that a literary essayist can annotate the text, marking parts that especially stand out and then revisiting those parts to ask, "Why did this stand out for me?"

On the other hand, when students write personal narrative entries, I might suggest they take a minute to think of a person (or place or thing) that matters to them and then list several times when they did something with that person (or in that place or with that thing). Then I would suggest they reread that list, select one episode that they remember with crystal clarity and that holds some significance, and begin to write the story of that one episode.

The important thing is that once kids have been taught a few strategies, they will begin developing a repertoire of genre-specific strategies for generating writing, and they can learn to draw on that repertoire to generate their own writing topics. They can also draw on that repertoire to generate more focused topics even when assigned a general one. That is, a researcher writing about teen activism still needs to generate his or her angled topic and can use the repertoire of generating strategies to do so. More than this, young people can learn that when they live as writers, the details of their lives and their thinking are worth developing. They learn to live (experiencing, observing, listening, reading) with a writer's consciousness, thinking, "I should write about this."

A big part of rehearsal involves generating ideas for writing.

Many people think of rehearsal as a time for writers to plan a draft before embarking on it, and it is true that planning is central to rehearsal. But especially when writers are given responsibility for generating topics for their writing, a big part of rehearsal involves gathering and choosing between ideas for writing.

Earlier, when discussing the use of writer's notebooks, I talked about the importance of teaching students to live writerly lives. If a person writes often, then rehearsal is not just a discrete activity one does at the desk just before embarking on a draft. It is also a sort of wide-awake way of living. When asked about the way that writing can alter a person's perception of his or her life, Katherine Paterson, the author of *Bridge to Terabithia*, told the story of her son David calling to her to come watch as a cicada shed its skin. As they crouched alongside the bug, they watched a tiny slit appear on the bug's back; as it was gradually pulled down as if the bug had a waist-length zipper, they saw a hint of color through the slit. Then there were more colors—aqua, yellow, green, cream, flecks of gold like jewelry on its head. Then the wings emerged, crumpled ribbons at first, then stretched out. As they watched, the cicada swung like an acrobat onto a new twig and then flew off, "oblivious to the wake of wonder it left behind." Paterson said, "As I let that wake of wonder wash over me, I realized that this was the real gift I want to give students, for what good are straight teeth and trumpet lessons to a person who cannot see the grandeur that the world is charged with?" (*Gates of Excellence: On Reading and Writing Books for Students*, 1981, 20).

Writer's notebooks support the consciousness Paterson believes is so critical to writing. When young people (and their teachers) carry notebooks (literally and figuratively) through their lives, this supports them in living with the perspective of being a writer, seeing potential stories, essays, and editorials everywhere. Writers notice something and think, "I should jot this down. I may want to make something of it." In time, students come to the writing workshop already knowing what they want to write, which suggests that they see potential stories and essays everywhere and also are able to select, from all the possibilities, ideas that seem to them to be worth developing and planning as a first draft.

This alertness to potential topics is absolutely essential to any writer who mines his or her life for potential writing topics, but it is also part of the process for writers who write about their research and reading. For example, once I had decided to write a book about the Common Core State Standards, you can be sure that I went through life living as a magnet on that topic. Anything that I read or heard or saw relating to that topic became grist for my writing mill. I knew that I needed to develop my own insights about and analysis of the CCSS, so I collected observations, recorded patterns, jotted down questions, and used this "great garage sale" of related junk to spark ideas and insights. As part of my rehearsal, I read over everything I had gathered and jotted insights such as "A surprising number of people regard papers such as 'A Publisher's Guide to the CCSS' or 'The Seven Shifts'—papers that reflect one organization's interpretation of the Common Core State Standards—as what the Common Core State Standards actually say. If people would only go back to the actual source, they'd realize that the CCSS and those documents differ in dramatic ways." Some insights I jotted ended up becoming central ideas, in which case I then gathered more facts to support that insight—again, living a writerly life, only this time with a more focused magnetic force. In the same way, a student researching the American Revolution will first collect insights and ideas related to that broad writing territory, and then when a more focused topic emerges, she will collect sources around that narrowed topic.

Rehearsal also involves weighing possible structures.

Of course, rehearsal for writing also involves imagining possible structures for a piece of writing and thinking about how one's content could fit into one structure, another, and another. "In my report on the Boston Tea Party, do I have enough information about the chronology of the event to write a chapter on the start of it, the middle of it, the ending of it, and the aftereffect? What if I lump together the ending and the aftereffect? Could I write about different subtopics instead? If so, what would they be? If I tried to write a subsection on the causes, do I have that information? What about a subsection on the people involved?"

As students work on their leads, their introductions, and their thesis statements, they try on different ways that their texts might go. You can teach writers that planning can involve drafting and revising leads or introductions or thesis statements. For example, I recommend that students who are writing narratives try writing a lead by mentally replaying the event and then capturing the initial actions or dialogue on the page, because writing a lead in this fashion helps writers envision and dramatize the unfolding story in ways that allow readers to experience that story. If a narrative writer decides that an orienting statement is needed at the very start of a story, I recommend he add that later. I recommend that information writers learn, eventually, to think of themselves as tour guides, taking readers on a tour of their topic, and to learn that an overview up front helps readers anticipate where the tour will lead. Of course, at first students will draft and revise alternative leads or introductions without realizing that in doing so, they are exploring alternative ways their entire texts might go.

With experience, everything students do one time during revision can move forward, becoming part of rehearsal.

As kids become more experienced and skilled as writers, everything they learn through revision can move forward into the rehearsal stage of their writing. For example, some writers begin the year writing about gigantic topics—"My trip to my grandma's house." Only during revision do these students reread their writing and think, "Which *particular aspect* of my visit do I want to address?" With experience, however, these same students will soon learn to generate focused ideas for writing and to screen those ideas, asking, "Will this story (essay, editorial, report) be focused enough?"

Similarly, the initial entries students write will not be detailed, nor will they be written in paragraphs, and so forth. As young people learn more and more, however, the work they do during rehearsal will incorporate features they earlier learned only through revision. These might include writing with details and paragraphing but may also include showing rather than telling, developing the heart of the story, including text citations, deliberately varying the kinds of supportive evidence used, or any one of a host of other skills. In other words, the more skilled and experienced a writer becomes, the more that writer can do during rehearsal.

Experienced writers are apt to do more—and spend longer—in rehearsal.

A professional writer might delay drafting for six months to a year, using this time to write and critique a whole sequence of different plans for a text! Such a writer would prefer progressing through multiple *outlines* rather than multiple *drafts*. A thirteen-year-old student, of course, will not find it easy to scrawl a few words onto the page and then look at this outline or plan, imagining from the abbreviated notes the larger text or the problems such a text might engender—let alone imagining another way that the text could have been written. Still, a thirteen-year-old can live like a writer, seeing potential for stories, arguments, and essays everywhere. A thirteen-year-old can use all she knows about good writing (or good narratives, good essays, and so on) to lift the level of her entries, thus giving her taller shoulders on which to stand when she selects one entry to develop into a major piece of writing. She can also learn to talk through the writing she plans to do, trying out one way and then another of approaching her subject, observing her audience's responses to those "in-the-air" drafts, and revising the drafts before she's even written a word.

And certainly, beginning middle school students can learn to make outlines, revising these in preparation for writing. They can look at a rough diagram of an editorial and think, "My last reason is sort of the same as the second one. I should make them more distinct from one another." They can realize the supporting information in their research report is not varied and set out to gather a wider variety. Then, too, they can look at a story mountain and think, "I need to really build up this part of my story. It is my rising action. I need to show how he tried, tried, tried." All of this can be done in preparation for writing a draft.

Drafting

While rehearsal and revision both involve the deliberate use of one strategy or another, drafting is less strategic. After all the work of collecting, choosing, planning, teaching others, storytelling, and imagining the piece laid out on the page, the writer takes pen in hand and writes.

For many writers, velocity is important when drafting. William Stafford describes writing this way: "When I write . . . I get pen and paper, take a glance out the window (often it is dark out there), and wait. It is like fishing. But I do not wait long, for there is always a nibble—and this is where receptivity comes in. To get started, I will accept anything that occurs to me. Something always occurs . . . If I put down something, that thing will help the next thing come, and I'm off. If I let the process go on, things will occur to me that were not at all in my mind when I started . . . For the person who follows with trust and forgiveness what occurs to him, the world remains always ready and deep, an inexhaustible environment" ("A Way of Writing," in *To Compose: Teaching Writing in High School and College*, 1990, 17–20).

When writing "fast and furious" or "strong and long," writers need to be positioned in ways that pay off for them. For a narrative writer, for example, it is helpful if the writer has made what I refer to as a "movie in the mind" and keeps her eye on that movie. Peter Elbow, the great writing teacher and author of *Writing with Power*, advises, "Don't *describe* the tree. *See* the tree!" He is not really saying anything different than I am when I suggest that writers make a movie in their mind and keep their eyes on that movie.

The larger point is actually not even about narrative writing. It is that powerful writing comes not from thinking about penmanship, word choice, complex sentences, and showing, not telling, as one writes. Powerful writing comes from being full of one's subject and keeping one's eye on that subject.

The essayist doesn't make a movie in his or her mind, but instead assumes a teaching/explaining/persuading stance, feels full of his or her subject, and then when putting pen to page, tries to write in ways that teach or persuade readers, as if those readers were standing before the writer.

Either way, one hopes that writers write quickly, knowing that writing a draft is playing in clay, not inscribing in marble, and that there will be time another day to roll up one's sleeves and revise. Writers are more willing to revise if the draft is written quickly—as a trial effort. Revision, then, becomes a time to see what the fast and furious writing yielded.

Revision

Writing is a powerful tool for capturing thought precisely because when a person writes, putting whatever occurs to her on the page, the writer can put those initial thoughts away, in a pocket or file, and on another day she can take them out to reread and rethink.

Over time, writers learn to re-see and reconsider first drafts through a variety of lenses. For starters, the writer pretends to be a stranger to these ideas, reading the draft as if encountering it for the first time, spying on her experience of the draft to imagine what a reader's experience of and reaction to it might be. Doing this, the writer is asking, "What will a reader make of this?" Are there sections that are unclear, claims that require more evidence? This sort of rereading can fuel powerful revisions.

Writers can also reread to consider a draft in light of his or her goals, asking, "Can I see the qualities of writing that I'm aiming to achieve in this text?" In other words, if a writer has studied effective essays and learned that essays often shift between precise examples and overarching ideas, the writer might look at her own essay and ask, "Does my essay shift between the general and the specific?"

If a writer has studied a mentor text, noting qualities that work well in it, the writer can say, "Let me see if I've brought that quality into this draft" and might locate places in the text where he or she could try that same effect. In a similar way, if a writer learns about—or hears about—a technique that other writers have used to good effect, revision can be a time to try bringing that same technique into one's own draft. "E. B. White suggests the final sentence in a paragraph is the most important and should propel the reader forward," the writer might state. "I'm going to reread my final sentences and see if I can make them stronger."

Writers can, more generally, reread their own writing, asking, "What works here that I can build on?" and "What doesn't work here that I can repair or eliminate?"

As students become more experienced as writers, more of their revision can happen in their mind's eye as they weigh one alternative against another. I find that at the start of sixth grade, revision work is just beginning to happen in the abstract. If a student wants to try alternative introductions, it is not absolutely necessary for the writer to literally write each alternative down on the page, as he may have needed to do in years prior. And certainly by the time students are in eighth grade, if they are experienced with the writing process, they will be able to do more revision by musing over questions and using predictable questions, fragments of writing, and notes to pin tentative ideas on the page, weighing those ideas against others. Your eighth-grader should become more skilled, as well, at capturing what he or she rehearses orally onto the page. Where you'll often see a big gap between what a sixth-grader says and then what he or she actually writes, there should be more convergence by eighth grade.

The most sophisticated and important sort of revision isn't fixing up one's text so that it works more effectively to convey one's meaning. Instead, the most sophisticated sort of revisions involves the writer looking *through his*

> *"As students become more experienced as writers, more of their revision can happen in their mind's eye as they weigh one alternative against another."*

draft to come to a deeper, more nuanced, more thoughtful understanding of his content. This sort of revision begins with the writer asking, "What am I trying to say?" and then revising to highlight that meaning. In time, this sort of revision becomes more exploratory. Writers venture into unexplored terrain and stumble on new insights that illuminate a topic not only for the reader but also for the writer. When a writer anticipates that he or she will revise to discover and clarify what the text is really saying, such a writer eventually drafts differently. For such writers, it can sometimes work to write without knowing exactly what it is they want to say, then write to figure out what they think.

Editing

Professional writers tend to postpone editing until the text is ready to be published. Like adult writers, young writers learn the value of writing rough drafts quickly, without pausing to use *Roget's Thesaurus* or spelling tools in the midst of drafting. And like adult writers, kids do not pore over a draft, worrying that every convention is correct, until it is time for the writing to be published. It's not a productive use of time to fix up writing that might change dramatically in revision. That's not to say that young writers don't automatically draw on their best knowledge of conventions as they draft. That's a given. But catching the small mistakes that you'll only notice when you are reading not for meaning but for conventions is something that's worth doing once you've clarified your meaning—which means working first on the structure and content of your draft.

Once the main structure and content of a draft have been revised so that the text feels stable, writers reread, checking each sentence, word, and letter. In middle school, students don't bring their own best efforts to teachers for a final check. They are responsible, and for this reason, many middle schoolers have learned to run drafts by someone else. Many also use the digital tools available. Some teachers ask students to refrain from fixing drafts using spell-check, until they have applied their knowledge of spelling patterns. That only makes sense if you are actively teaching spelling patterns. Students can also check their spelling by drawing on their knowledge of root words, prefixes, and suffixes. When words have been misspelled, the most important thing is that the writer senses this—perhaps writing words that seem off several times in the margins of their paper, working to figure out which of the spellings is the more conventional. All of this practice aims to help students improve their spelling skills over time. While a lot of the high-stakes writing they'll do

will be on word-processing tools that will have spell-checkers and grammar checkers, some won't, and middle school students are still young. They can still improve their knowledge of spelling if you and they give some time to it.

Editing, however, involves much more than correcting spelling, and you will want to teach students to check for the grammar and conventions that you've taught. That probably means checking that they've included ending punctuation, that their verb tenses agree, that they've used commas for internal punctuation, that their pronoun references are clear, that they've punctuated dialogue, quotes, and citations accurately. They'll probably need a "cheat sheet" of exemplars to check their work against. "Does this sound right?" will work well with students who are immersed in and out of school in academic English. For those who may not be, they'll need concrete examples to compare their work to.

You will teach editing during minilessons and also within mid-workshop teachings, share sessions, and homework assignments. Obviously, you will tailor your lessons so they are roughly aligned with what most of the class needs, using small-group instruction to provide special support for students who need it. As the year unfolds, your writers will have access to a growing list of skills. *The Power of Grammar*, by Mary Ehrenworth and Vicki Vinton (2005), lays out methods and curriculum for teaching grammar inside of writing workshop. *Catching Up on Conventions*, by Elisa Zonana and Chantal Francois (2009), offers tips and tools for designing exercises, small-group lessons, and homework for students who are not immersed in academic English outside of school. The key thing to remember is that writers can only edit for skills they have been taught. You can't expect them to intuit the conventions of academic English just by reading.

Once students have been taught to edit with particular concerns in mind, then those skills and strategies need to move forward in the writing process, becoming part of the writer's repertoire of skills that he draws on while scrawling a rough draft. So while you will not want your students to fret about writing perfectly correct drafts, it will also not be helpful for them to postpone all thought of spelling and punctuation until the final throes of working on a manuscript. Over time, you will want your students to be able to use mostly correct spelling and punctuation and paragraphing even when they write very fast rough drafts. And punctuation cannot be an afterthought, inserted into a manuscript just before it goes to press! So you will channel your students to take a few minutes as they write their rough drafts to make sure that the conventions they "almost know" are under control. Then, during editing, you can encourage students to reexamine conventions that pose problems for them, relying on resources and one another to edit these problematic areas.

Once a student has edited her own writing, you may want to confer with the writer, teaching her another few strategies she can use to edit the text. Perhaps the student will have added quotation marks correctly but will have not yet mastered the punctuation that accompanies quotations. In the editing conference, you can support that student's use of quotation marks and show the student the next step toward correct handling of quotations. In your editing conference, you might go over one quote with the student and then ask her to read through the draft, fixing other quotations in a similar way. Meanwhile, however, there will be some incorrect spellings and some problems with verb tenses, and you might choose not to tackle those. That is, in editing conferences, like in every other kind of conference, a teacher makes a choice, teaching the student a few things that seem to be within his reach. Pull a few students alongside as you teach this conference, as it will undoubtedly benefit them as well.

Before the student's work is published, some middle school teachers wonder if they should go through the final draft as a copy editor would, correcting it. This final step calls for a decision. If you correct the students' final work before it is published, then that text will be easier for others to read. On the other hand, if you do this, then the student's final work does not really reflect what the learner can do independently, and it will be harder for you to hold yourself to being sure that students are growing in their abilities to correct their own writing. Consider with your students when the writing is high stakes enough, and the publishing is public enough, that they want to run their final draft past a copy editor. Some teachers assemble some copy editors, which might include you, might include some parents, or might include some students who are skilled at conventions and spelling. It is helpful to instill in some of your students that even when they have done their very best to spell and punctuate well, they'll still want to run high-stakes writing past someone who will act as an editor.

Cycling through the Entire Process

Just as students need to have a sense of how a narrative or an argument or an information text tends to go, they need to have a sense of how the process of writing that kind of text is apt to go. For example, you don't want the stage of gathering entries, doing research, developing reasons, and collecting evidence to be so long that kids can't feel that it is just a prelude to framing an argument. The gathering of entries and collecting of information can't feel like an end in itself. Students need to plan and draft their writing, anticipating the day they'll revise it and, better yet, anticipating the day they'll send the text out into the world. When I am creating a version of the writing process for a class, I look for indications that the version of the writing process that I imagine for them matches what they can do with only a little support. I want to see that kids are productive, engaged, and purposeful throughout the entire process.

Chapter 5

Provisioning a Writing Workshop

Y EARS AGO, when I wrote the first edition of the now classic *The Art of Teaching Writing* (1994), I emphasized the importance of keeping workshops simple and predictable. Although my thinking on many things has changed over all these years, this injunction continues to be an important one, whether the workshop is a sixth-grade one or occurs in a graduate class. Back then, I wrote:

> If the writing workshop is always changing, always haphazard, students remain pawns waiting for their teacher's agenda. For this reason and others, I think it is important for each day's workshop to have a clear, simple structure. Children should know what to expect. This allows them to carry on; it frees the teacher from choreographing activities and allows time for listening. How we structure the workshop is less important than that we structure it. (25–26)

> I used to think that to teach creative writing I needed to have a creative management system. I thought creative environments, by definition, were ever changing, complex, and stimulating. Every day my classroom was different: one day we wrote for ten minutes, another day, not at all; sometimes students exchanged papers, and other days they turned them in; sometimes they published their writing, sometimes they didn't. My classroom was a whirlwind, a kaleidoscope, and I felt very creative. Rightly so. My days were full of planning, scheming, experimenting, replanning. Meanwhile my students waited on my changing agendas. They could not develop their own rhythms and strategies because they were controlled by mine. They could not plan, because they never knew what tomorrow would hold. They could only wait.

> I have finally realized that the most creative environments in our society are not the kaleidoscopic environments in which everything is always changing and complex. They are, instead, the predictable and consistent ones: the scholar's library, the researcher's laboratory, the artist's studio. Each of these environments is deliberately kept predictable and simple because the work at hand and the changing interactions around that work are so unpredictable and complex. (12)

To teach writing, you need to establish an environment and structures that will last throughout every day of your teaching. The essential premise, one that undergirds any writing workshop, is this: the writing workshop needs to be simple and predictable enough that your students can learn to carry on within it independently. In middle school in particular, so much changes for students as they move from one class to another, from one teacher to another, from one subject to another. Developing predictable structures will maximize your instructional time and your writers' time to work, and will provide them with a sense of continuity from one day to the next in an often otherwise fragmented school day.

Because the work of writing is complex and varied, because students need to be able to follow their texts toward meaning, and because you need, above all, to be able to coach writers who are engaged in the ongoing work of writing, the writing workshop in most classrooms proceeds in a similar way through a similar schedule, using similar room arrangements and materials regardless of the age of writers. My graduate classrooms will look similar to your eighth-grade classrooms in the essentials. It may seem like a small decision, what writing workshop will look and feel like, but managing a writing workshop becomes infinitely easier if students are taught in similar ways through succeeding years, thus allowing them to grow accustomed to the systems and structures of workshop teaching. In this chapter, I describe, in depth, a workshop environment that is predictable and structured and that allows for student independence. Because middle school classrooms vary tremendously in terms of their size, technology, and setup, I'll describe what we've found, in working with thousands of teachers around the country, to be an optimal setup, and then I'll also describe compromises and choices that let you teach workshop even if your constraints limit your options.

THE ENVIRONMENT FOR WRITING INSTRUCTION

Teaching writing does not require elaborate materials or special classroom arrangements. Teachers who teach in widely divergent ways can all offer students direct instruction in good writing. There are, however, a few room arrangements that especially support the teaching of writing, and you may want to consider arranging your classroom around the shared principles described in the following section. You may also want to consider provisioning your classroom with the materials that will make a big difference in your students' energy and willingness to write, outlined later in the chapter.

Room Arrangements

If I were to take you on a tour of any one of the thousands of schools where writing workshops flourish, you'd notice distinctive room arrangements. In each classroom, you would see a meeting area, a workspace, and writing tools and resources space.

The Meeting Area: A Space to Convene

Middle school teachers often worry about whether it is possible and doable for them to convene their students for minilessons. As I prepared this book for press, I met with all the middle school staff developers at the Teachers College Reading and Writing Project to get a final consensus opinion on this issue and a few others like it. "When going to press with books that will reach the whole country, how strongly do we want to press for teachers to pull their students into a meeting area?" I asked. Every member of our team was adamant that I should push hard for middle school teachers to find a way to convene their classes. And every member of the team urged me to point out to you that this is entirely doable in the real world of middle schools.

In many middle schools, teachers keep two benches under the whiteboard at the front of the room, and when it is time for a minilesson, those benches get spread apart just a bit, with chairs at either end, to form a simple sort of a meeting area. In other rooms, a stack of carpet tiles allows for students to clump together. These simple ways to convene students can make a big difference in the tone, efficiency, and efficacy of middle school workshop. Gathering middle school students into some kind of meeting area defines when you are in a minilesson, versus when you release students to work independently. Pulling and then releasing kids from the meeting area thus acts as a metaphor for when you want kids to pay attention to you, and when they need to pay attention to their own work. Second, pulling kids into a meeting area accentuates the atmosphere of intimacy and trust that is crucial to successful writing workshops. You need to develop a community of writers who work closely together, writing about topics they care enormously about, trusting each other with the details of these topics. It is hard to do that if you are broadcasting your voice to kids at the back of the room. Thirdly, pulling kids so they are more to the front increases kids' ability to see and hear and thus increases engagement and maximizes achievement. Recruiting kids' attention is not easy, but it is vastly easier when you pull them together for a ten-minute minilesson. They're willing to give you ten minutes of tight, focused attention.

Some of you, I know, teach in tiny rooms where it's hard to imagine a meeting area. Others of you teach in rooms that are large, but there are so many adolescent bodies, so many clunky old desks with arms, that it equally feels hard to make a meeting area. Because the metaphoric act of pulling and releasing attention matters so much, teachers with whom we work have found ways to create the feel of a meeting area in even the most inhospitable of spaces. As mentioned earlier, sometimes all we can do is to organize a way for the very back row or two of kids to slide forward. Sometimes they slide chairs forward; sometimes they sit on their desks briefly. The five seconds it takes them to take their places and then leave them will actually help define the parts of your workshop.

Remember that you can turn this problem over to your students. Tell them that in graduate writing classes, writers try to have a place where they can come together to study mentor texts, listen closely to writing, and work together on new strategies. Then writers need space to go off to work. Put the challenge into your students' hands, invite them to ask families for benches, carpets, and milk crates, and see what you can do.

I once watched Elisa Zonana, a literacy coach who really believed in the value of meeting areas, go into a ninth-grade classroom, where the teacher was sure she couldn't make a meeting area, and within five minutes, Elisa had gotten the kids to figure it out, had them practice coming and going and moving their chairs, and at the same time, gotten the kids invested in it.

Of course, while working to finesse reasonable compromises you will also want to keep in mind an image of the ideal situation. Certainly in scores of classrooms a large carpet (nine by twelve feet) occupies one corner of the classroom, framed with bookcases, and this centers a meeting space. You'll be surprised at how many middle school students are happy to sit on the floor for ten minutes—and you'll be able to host small groups there as well. Usually, one corner of this carpet features a stool or chair for you. Always, teaching equipment will be nearby the chair, including, hopefully, a document camera or Smart Board hooked up to a laptop, and also an easel with chart paper, markers, and a fine-tipped pointer. Sometimes you may write on the computer, other times on paper. There are times when your document camera or Smart Board will serve you well, and other times when you *don't* want to create that feel of a college seminar; you want the quickness and informality of jotting in front of the kids, or of unveiling a teaching chart bit by bit. Ideally, you have both access to technology and access to paper.

Regardless of whether your charts are paper or digital, you will want to create teaching charts. Middle school writers need records in the room of the things they have learned to do—these tools support their agency. These are described in more detail later. See the section dedicated to charts later on in this chapter for more detailed information.

> "Recruiting kids' attention is not easy, but it is vastly easier when you pull them together for a ten-minute minilesson."

It's not only charts that need to be available, but also published texts and examples of student work and your demonstration texts. Again, it is helpful if there are small copies of these that students can insert into their writing notebooks if they choose to do so. Often these are featured on bulletin boards, but it is also important for teachers to have a way to draw attention to particular aspects of texts during whole-class study.

The Common Core State Standards' emphasis on close reading and evidenced-based instruction has made it all the more important for students to be able to make specific references to a text while discussing it. To help the class study texts closely, teachers try to have a document camera, an overhead projector, or a Smart Board nearby during minilessons, with a ready wall or screen on which to project the enlarged text. It is very inconvenient to move tables and chairs each time a projector is needed, so you'll see that in most classrooms a permanent lodging spot has been found for the equipment, one that doesn't require a lot of reshuffling to access and use it. For example, an overhead projector is often on a low table alongside the easel, angled toward the wall.

Throughout the writing workshop, it is important for students to sit alongside assigned writing partners. During minilessons, you will often ask students to practice something quickly with another student, and a pair saves a lot of time if it is clear who each student is talking to. You will want to develop stable, consistent seating during the minilesson and also during the writing workshop to minimize transition time and maximize engagement. Keep in mind that the kids who choose to sit in the back and outer edges of the meeting area and the kids who choose to sit front and center will probably need to be reversed! Put your strongest students—the ones who find it easy to pay attention—on your perimeter. Put your more reluctant writers right at your feet. Literally. It is helpful if one partner is named Partner 1, and the other, Partner 2, so that when you want to assign tasks rapidly during the minilesson, you are able to say, "Partner 1, you'll listen for . . . Partner 2, you . . ."

Work Areas: Space for Writing and Conferring

Although the meeting space is important in these classrooms, the most important thing is the rhythm of students pulling close around the teacher for a short stretch of clear, explicit instruction, followed by them dispersing to their work places, with the teacher now meeting with individuals and small groups as students write. That is, the rhythm in a writing classroom is not three minutes in which the teacher talks, elicits, and assigns; five minutes in which students work; then three more minutes in which the teacher again talks and assigns, followed by five more minutes of "seat work"; nor is it thirty minutes of a teacher talking and ten minutes of kids working. Instead, writing teachers teach explicitly for approximately ten minutes, and then students disperse to work on their writing for forty minutes.

It is critical, then, to think about room arrangements that can support students working for long stretches of time and that will allow you to move among the students to confer.

In our dream setup, middle school students can work at tables or at desks clustered together to form table-like seating arrangements. If you're really lucky, they each have a notebook *and* an iPad or laptop that is connected to wireless printers . . . but that's still a dream for most classrooms. During writing time, students generally sit beside their writing partner. Partnerships typically last across a unit of study and are then renegotiated. In general, writers benefit from quiet as they write, so you want students to have enough space around them that they are not distracted by lots of other students at their elbow. In this day and age, it is hard to ever achieve total quiet, so you may have writers who prefer to have headphones on, or you may play some quiet music. Figure this out with your class. Writers the world over need to make their own "cabin in the woods," and it will help your students if they learn to create a replicable environment in which they can get a lot of writing done. It will also benefit them if they can learn to work productively in the company of their friends, so that they can form study groups outside of school in middle and high school. Your classroom is the incubator for those habits.

Of course, you can teach writing well while maintaining a whole array of different room arrangements. So although I recommend that you cluster desks in table-like formations and distribute them around the room, leaving maximum space between the tables, you can certainly make other choices. I do not, however, recommend that you line desks up into two or three long lines, which makes it almost impossible for you to ever come alongside a student, to sit shoulder to shoulder with that student, or to achieve that atmosphere of agency and trust that is the key to successful workshop.

Materials

When a school decides to spotlight the teaching of writing, the good news is that this doesn't require a whole new cycle of budgets. A teacher really doesn't need much to teach writing beyond paper, pens, and storage containers. For technology, a lot of states have gone to "bring your own device," so that the classroom only needs to provide a few laptops. If you don't have great tech, don't despair. You can create powerful writers with old school pens and paper. Keyboarding is not the mark of strong writing; it's just one tool that makes it easier now. We've taught writing in parts of the world where there is no Internet or even electricity. The beauty of teaching writing is that you don't need to spend money. Other curricular initiatives often involve an enormous outlay of funds for a whole raft of new supplies, but reform in writing can proceed even if students sit on dirt floors and write on recycled paper.

The interesting thing about materials for writing is that although writing instruction does not require fancy materials, the flip side of this is also true. Materials can make an exponential difference. There's hardly a writer on earth who doesn't have a fetish of some sort about the kind of pen or notebook or lined paper or font size or software program that allows his or her juices to flow. And I have never known a writing teacher who doesn't use new tools as lures to help break down patterns of writing resistance.

So I do recommend that if you can do so, ask families, students, or your parent organization to contribute toward a kitty that will fund the supplies your students will like (even if they aren't essential) for your workshop. You can then take advantage of bulk prices.

When provisioning the classroom, you will certainly need to think about providing students with writer's notebooks, a way to store finished and ongoing work that happens outside the notebook, writing utensils and revision tools, writing partners, chart paper and markers, display materials, resources, and the special equipment that you may want to use for particular purposes at particular times. If your classroom is a totally digital one, you'll need to provide access to iPads or laptops, and printers.

Writer's Notebooks

The writer's notebook is a metaphor for the place where you are working on your writing. For us, as adults, it's now often a laptop, though many adults prefer the initial scrawl of pen on paper. Your students will be taking the SATs digitally, and perhaps your Common Core state exams digitally, and gradually, like us, they'll become writers who compose at a word processor. Certainly they'll be turning in most of their writing typed. That means you may decide to make the entire writing process digital, which means that kids will keep files and folders of their writing, saving entries and drafts digitally just as they would in a paper notebook.

There is, however, still something highly efficient and effective about paper notebooks. Kids can easily see what they've been doing, you can see it, and no one has to depend on digital prowess, access, or funding. You can say, "Flip through your notebook to see how much writing you've done over the last three days," and you can suggest students "look back at the work you were doing two days ago." It's not this mess of "find the file, oh-no-you-deleted-it-and-oh-you-replaced-it-with-your-next-day's-writing." Also, if your students ever want to write in places where they can't depend on digital access, you'll know they can do it. Whether they work with the Peace Corps, become a foreign correspondent, or survive in the postapocalyptic Hunger Games era, you and they will know they can still write.

Many schools order a writer's notebook for each student; in other schools, teachers show students a variety of optional notebooks and then ask them to purchase their own. They are both viable options, and that lets you also have some kids on iPads as needed. You will probably want to steer students away from spiral notebooks, because they have a "required class work" feel. You're going after a more magical feeling. Ideally a writer's notebook gives the impression that it could have been the notebook of choice for one of the authors whom a student loves most. Another reason to avoid spiral notebooks, I think, is that some students (and some parents) have come to associate spiral notebooks full of writing with student journals, and there is a world of difference between what most people mean by the term *journal* and what your students are doing. Journals are often containers for writing that has no genre and no audience (other than perhaps the teacher) and that is never revised, edited, or published.

It is also perfectly acceptable for writer's notebooks to be very simple (the marble-covered composition books readily available at stores everywhere work fine for a notebook), especially if the writer personalizes it. Sometimes writers laminate a collage of pictures and words of wisdom onto the covers. Encourage your students to write messages such as "If lost, return to So-and-So" inside the cover of the notebook. Personalizing the cover of a notebook and writing notes that will help a student retrieve a lost notebook are ways to support the bonding process that is so essential. This emotional attachment matters more than one might imagine.

Whether their notebooks are digital or paper, kids will date each entry they write. Writing that is done outside the notebook also needs to be dated and saved. That way, you and your students can readily see the amount of writing a student has done in a day or during a week, and trace growth, revision, and experimentation. If some kids keep digital notebooks, make sure they don't replace their writing with newer versions each day—insist they save their files so they can sometimes print or lay them out and look at change and growth.

In many classrooms, teachers suggest that the final fifth of a paper notebook be reserved for the student and the teacher to write about goals, assessments, plans, strategies, and the like. Students can tape checklists into this section and write about the goals they set for themselves and the ways they can go about meeting those goals. Teachers can record plans that are made in conferences, and use this as a place to hold students accountable to meeting those plans. If kids are in digital notebooks, Evernote works well as a site for keeping all of these materials.

It may be a challenge to teach some students to carry their notebooks (or folders) with them between home and school, not leaving their writing materials (and their writing) at home. You can expect that during one of the first few days of the year, you will encounter a student who says, "I left my notebook at home." If you comfort the writer with "That's okay. Just write on notebook paper and tape it into your notebook tomorrow," you will soon find that half that class has left their writing at home. So brace yourself. You are going to need to make this a capital offense and you are going to have to help kids problem solve! Beforehand, practice in front of a mirror so that you are ready to display to the whole class your dismay with the discovery that some-one has left his or her notebook at home. (Sure, you realize half the class has done this, but don't let on, and the culprits will feel as if they have narrowly escaped with their lives!) One approach is to say in a voice that is kind but easily overheard. "*Wow*, this is a crisis for you. How will you keep going? How will you build on the writing work you've started?" Then wait until the room is quiet enough for everyone to hear a pin drop. Ask, "Is your mother or father at home, so if you call, one of them can bring it over? No—they're working? They get a mid-morning break, perhaps? Maybe we could get one of them to leave work to swing by and get it . . ."

Now, of course, you do not really mean to phone this student's parent and suggest that she leave work to bring her daughter's notebook to the classroom. But the point is that if you play this right, you can communicate that it is a very big deal to forget one's notebook. Another approach is to pull in the writer's partner. "You need to figure this out together. We have to be like the Marines—we leave no one behind. So Steven, it's not enough that you have your notebook. Tomorrow, you need to help Martin have his too. So will you call? Will you text?" That evening, the whole class can rally to text each other, reminding partners to bring their notebooks next day.

When all else fails, you may end up with one or two students who need to leave their notebooks in school, and staple paper in each day that they wrote on at home. The rest, though, you want to coach, harass, and support into the habits that will let them be successful.

Writing-in-Progress Folders and Paper and Publication Tools

In addition to a writer's notebook, each student will need a folder for drafts—again, either a paper folder or a digital folder. Sometimes a student's writing is kept in her writer's notebook and sometimes in her folder, depending on the nature of the writing. Either way, it is crucial that the work is dated each day—perhaps with that day's date stamp. This makes it easy for you to look through a student's notebook and folder to re-create what the student did in the writing workshop on Monday, Tuesday, Wednesday, and so on. Principals often sit down with writing folders as part of their supervision and want to see evidence of students' ongoing work.

Writing folders contain drafts and mentor texts related to the current unit of study. They may or may not contain checklists in which students self-assess as well as goal sheets. Most of the teachers I know suggest using a two-pocket folder for storing these materials. Usually, during the first week or two of the unit, students will do most of their writing in their writer's notebooks, and during the second half of the unit they will do most of their writing on draft paper that they keep in their folders, or they begin drafting digitally. If they draft digitally, they can use the comment function in Word or Google Docs to annotate their writing as they go, and to respond to each other's writing—again, making sure they save multiple drafts so you and they can trace their revision progress.

In middle schools in the United States, most writing students publish will be typed, though you may sometimes have an informal publishing along the way where it's not worth it for your students to type their pieces. Expect that you'll have to demonstrate some of the keyboarding techniques that allow students to indent paragraphs, format fonts, and so on. Tuck this in as you are demonstrating, and it will become an along-the-way part of writing. In other places around the world where we teach, especially places where not only technology but paper is limited, students may keep adding to their original draft and never recopy it. That is far from advisable, but also not the end of the world. The point is the quality of the final piece, not its format. Keep your mind on bringing up flexible, resilient writers who can write in any circumstances.

Charts

One of the big goals of your teaching will be to help your students develop a growing repertoire of skills and strategies that they learn to draw on delib-erately as they pursue their own important purposes. This means that it is incumbent on you to make your teaching have sticking power. In workshop classrooms, most teachers have found that they can use classroom charts to emphasize that students should continually draw from their growing reper-toire of strategies. You can make these charts by hand, or you can project them on a screen, or you can print them out. They can be large in size, or they can be small. The main chart that threads through a unit of study is referred to as an "anchor chart." If you teach two information writing units—say, one at the start of the year in which students write about topics of personal interest and then one later in the year in which kids write about a discipline-based topic—the anchor chart from the first information writing unit will resurface in the second. Sometimes anchor charts even travel from one grade level to the next, with teachers saying to eighth-graders, for example, "Last year you learned lots of ways to angle your text evidence." After referencing the chart that accompanied that teaching, the teacher might say, "Would you look at the essay you just wrote and see how many of last year's techniques you remembered to use this year?"

Each unit's anchor chart will be prominently displayed. Often there is an envelope near a chart containing small replicas of the chart. Students are encouraged to tape a miniature chart into their notebooks or their desks portfolio.

If you have the opportunity to visit a lot of middle school ELA classrooms, you will probably find, as we have found, that there often aren't enough records of teaching in the room to support the students' drawing on and using prior instruction. Sometimes the charts that are there are very summary-like, not providing students with tools that remind them of the strategies they have been taught and not providing examples of what good work entails. It is helpful to post your demonstration text or student exemplars next to your charts. If you are able to park some kids in front of a chart and say "Here, do it like that . . . ," then you can be confident that your chart is an effective one. Here are some suggestions about charts:

- Make charts with your students—if not the whole chart, then a part so that they will take ownership and remember the content.

- Make sure the heading names a big skill or goal so that students know the purpose of the chart.

- Use visuals (photos, icons, exemplars) so all kinds of learners are able to get a lot of information at a glance.

- Consider making charts interactive. For example, ask kids to add their names (on sticky notes) next to strategies tried, or have strategies written on sticky notes that can be borrowed as needed, or post exemplars alongside a label for it.

- Talk about charts often with the whole class, small groups, and partnerships.

- Periodically revise charts, condense them, or retire them. And then pull them out in fresh circumstances.

You will also have one-day charts in your writing workshop. For example, in a unit of study on writing literary essays, you might quickly jot some of the theories that your seventh-graders are considering as they develop their literary essays. That chart is apt to remain up for a day or two. The one-day charts will not represent cumulative teaching points from across a large swath of the unit.

A note about charts in middle school classrooms that are highly digital. The digital revolution has been marvelous for middle school kids. More kids are writing than ever before (even if a lot of it is social media!); access to technology has helped with engagement for some students, and with modifications for others. Smart Boards and projectors and Google Docs make it easy for teachers and kids to see each other's work, give feedback, and feel connected as writers. There are two things to watch for, though. One is that while you say to yourself that you will print out that screenshot of your teaching, the one with the clear description of the strategy and the teacher demonstration text, you forget to do so, or when you go to do it the printer doesn't work, or if it works, it's out of paper. Days go by, and kids have no record of recent instruction. Then you get worried and you start having kids copy everything that is up on the screen. Now twenty minutes go by, and kids are using up their writing energy, copying the minilesson. Not good! So the first thing to be aware of in a high-tech classroom, is how you are being innovative (or old-school) in getting records of instruction up in the room and into kids' hands so they can lean on these crucial tools. The second thing to watch for is an overdependence on technology—one that leaves you in a teaching crisis if the machines don't work (because often, they won't).

Exemplar Texts

Writers need to read widely, deeply, ravenously, and closely. A classroom full of powerful writers is one in which teachers read aloud often and bring in texts to share with the class, and with particular students, Although students benefit from a rich classroom and school libraries full of a great variety of texts, to learn to write well, they especially need to read texts that resemble those they are trying to write. And they need to not only graze these texts but also study some of them incredibly closely, revisiting them time and again to learn still more and more. The same text can be used to teach leads, endings, elaboration, sentence structure, literary or rhetorical devices, and a dozen other things. I've often led workshops for teachers in which I show how one single text can be the source for dozens of minilessons. This means, then, that each teacher needs a short stack of highly engaging and closely studied short texts that students return to over and over throughout the year. For some of these texts, you'll want your kids to have access to print or digital copies, so that they can use them at home, bring out in a small group or partnership, and underline and annotate. You might have one or two texts that reappear across grade levels—and if so, you and your colleagues will want to consider which new techniques will be highlighted each year.

> "Managing middle school students so they work with independence and rigor is a very big deal, and decisions you make about your room arrangements and materials can play an important part in this."

Tools to Support Spelling and Language Growth

You'll have students who encode easily, learning spelling of difficult words from the texts they read and your models, and you'll have students for whom spelling is tough. For students whose spelling doesn't rise to the level of their content, you'll want to think about the kinds of spelling approaches that may be helpful, and think about how you'll help them make time to do this work. In general, dictionaries are not actually helpful, as they were intended as a way for people to find the meaning of words they already know how to spell. There are, now, phonetic dictionaries, and apps that let kids say a word and then get the spelling—these might be helpful coping devices for some of your students.

If your students still struggle over high-frequency words, it is especially important that you help them address this problem. Fifty percent of the words that students write are the same thirty-six words! You can recognize that a student has trouble with high-frequency words when you see the writer spell a word like *constitution* correctly, after learning that word in Social Studies, and then misspell *because*. On the Teachers College Reading and Writing Project website, http://readingandwritingproject.com, (Google search "Reading and

Writing Project reading assessments"), you can find lists of high-frequency words. The lists are arranged in order by frequency and difficulty. Clearly you will want students to start with the earliest list on which they miss words, make a plan to learn them, and proceed from there.

Kids will also need to learn technical or academic language—ones you'll introduce within certain units of study, like *narrative*, *rhetoric*, or *fallacy*. These words, you'll want to display in the room. Thesauruses will also be helpful for kids as they explore more literary language. Have on hand some print thesauruses, make sure the thesaurus application is enabled on their word-processing programs, and perhaps have visual-thesaurus.com (Google search term visual thesaurus) available on a class computer. Show, when you are demonstrating, how you sometimes turn to these tools. Kids love words, and they'll learn new ones every time they write when it's easy for them to play with language.

Of course, many students will rely on technology to help them fix up their spelling, and this is a great coping strategy. They still want to work at improving their spelling along the way, balancing the energy they give this with the energy they put into becoming overall stronger writers. Remember, no one says of Hemingway "what a great speller he was!" You can be a poor speller and a good writer. You can be a poor speller and be successful. So make spelling one small part of the ongoing work of becoming an ever-stronger writer.

Don Murray, the godfather of writing workshop, writes that writers need only three things: time, choice, and response. They need protected time to write, they need choice over what they write about, and they need response from readers and other writers. They don't need stuff. They don't need copy machines or color printers or fancy projectors or the latest laptop. All of those things are lovely, but all your writers really need is something to write with and something to write on, access to mentor texts and expert instruction, and a place to work.

Because writers don't need much, it is entirely possible for a school system to provision writing workshops with all that is needed, and doing so is enormously important—don't make it hard for kids to write because they don't have time, space, or materials. I've watched writing workshops take hold within a year or two in classrooms up and down the corridors of a school, and when I try to discern the conditions that made it likely for teachers and students to embrace the writing workshop, one remarkable feature stands out: *the essentials were available*. What those essentials mean will shift over time. Throughout the history of the human race, tools have made us smarter. The wheel, the stylus, the computer—these tools of the hand become habits of the mind, re-creating what it means to live and learn together. Teachers and school leaders, too, are wise to pay attention to the important work of provisioning writing workshops.

As described in more detail in the next chapter, managing middle school students so they work with independence and rigor is a very big deal, and decisions you make about your room arrangements and materials can play an important part in this. Even if your entire focus is on explicit teaching, bear in mind that unless your students can sustain work with some independence, you will not be free to teach. How important it is, then, for you to take seriously the structuring of your writing workshop.

Chapter 6

Structures and Management Systems

T O TEACH WRITING, you need to establish the structures and expectations that ensure that all students will continue working throughout the writing workshop on their own important writing projects. Otherwise, your entire attention will be focused on keeping kids working—and you therefore won't be able to devote yourself to the all-important work of assessing, coaching, scaffolding, and teaching. Yet teaching young people to work hard with independence is no small feat!

You can start by recognizing that you need to give careful thought to how you will institute the systems that make it likely that your students will sustain rigorous work. When you plan your writing instruction, you will want to plan not only the words you will say—the minilessons and the conferences that will convey content about good writing—but also the management structures and systems that make it possible for middle school students to carry on as writers, working productively with independence and rigor. When workshops have clear and consistent structures and systems, teachers are freed from choreography and are able to teach.

Why do so many people assume that classroom management is a concern for novice teachers but not for master teachers? Is there really a good teacher anywhere who doesn't continually think hard about methods for maximizing students' productivity, for inspiring the highest possible work ethic, and for holding every learner accountable to doing his or her best? Who *doesn't* have trouble with classroom management? How could it *not* be tricky to build an environment in which thirty adolescents each pursues his or her own important project as a writer, working within the confines of a crowded room, each needing his or her own mix of silence and collaboration, time and deadlines, resources and one another?

Corporate management is considered an executive skill, and high-level executives are often coached in methods for maximizing productivity. Directors, managers, and executives attend seminars on developing systems of accountability, on providing feedback, on organizing time, space, and personnel to maximize productivity. If the people working under your direction were grown-ups instead of students, the job of management would be regarded as highly demanding leadership work.

As a classroom teacher, you absolutely need to give careful attention to methods of managing young people so they can sustain high levels of purposeful work. You and your colleagues would be wise to assume from the start that classroom management will be a challenge and to give careful thought to instituting systems that channel your students to do their best work.

The good news is that you needn't invent systems *ex nihilo*. Thousands of teachers have worked for decades to develop clear and consistent structures and systems that can free you from constant choreography and allow you to teach.

STRUCTURES AND SYSTEMS THAT FREE TEACHERS TO TEACH

I recently visited the classroom of first-year middle school teacher Patrice. The writing workshop was about to begin. "Writers," Patrice said, "come to the meeting area with your materials. You know what you need." Behind her was a small cue that I saw some students glance at, a mini-chart that said, *Writers bring essential materials with them to the lesson,* under which was written *writer's notebook, pen or pencil, current draft, your partner.* As she counted quietly backward ("Five, four, three, two, one"), I saw her signal to one student that she was forgetting her notebook by tapping her own, and wink at another who went back to grab a pen. A third of her students stayed in their seats, while most of the others tucked themselves into the front on the floor and a bench, and a few others moved up in back to sit on desks.

Patrice took her place on a stool by the front. "Writers," she said, "I'll know you're ready when your eyes are on me." Almost every kid sat up straighter and turned toward her. A few nudged their partners. Patrice then began a ten-minute minilesson in which she named a strategy that writers often use, demonstrated that strategy, gave students a few minutes of guided practice with the strategy, and invited her writers to add that strategy to their repertoire. At the end of her lesson, Patrice's kids made quick plans—they told their partners the specific work they would try to accomplish that day, and as each partnership was ready, they dispersed to their writing spots. Patrice kept a few writers in the meeting area to meet with her, saying "Emily, Will, Sarah, stay here, I've been thinking about you as writers and there is something I want to show you." Within a moment, students were dispersed to their writing spots, each hard at work on his or her ongoing writing. None of them required Patrice to come to their side and provide a personalized jump start.

As I watched all this, I marveled that Patrice, a novice teacher, was teaching in such efficient and effective ways. I remembered with a pang my first years as a teacher. How did she get to be so good? I wondered, but then I knew. Patrice is the teacher she is because although *she* is new to the profession, *her methods* are not new. Her methods have gone through hundreds of drafts and have benefited from the legacy of experienced teachers. This is how it should be! In any profession, we learn from those who have been in the field.

The best way I know to learn classroom management strategies is to visit well-established writing workshops to study the infrastructure that underlies this kind of teaching. Across the country, and around the globe, there are thousands of flourishing middle school writing workshops in public and independent schools. When you visit these classrooms, whether you drop in on Nature Hill or Silverlake Middle School in Oconomowoc, Wisconsin, or Tompkins Square Middle School in Manhattan, or KIPP RISE in Newark, or Colegio Nueva Granada in Bogotá, or the Singapore American School, you'll see that these writing workshops are structured in clear and consistent ways—the infrastructure is the same. In this chapter, you and I will visit some middle school writing workshops when they're in full swing, and we'll pay special attention to the nitty-gritty of classroom management. I'll be at your side on this tour, commenting on what we see together. We'll pay special attention to the management of each component of the writing workshop.

- Managing the minilesson: the beginning of each day's writing instruction

- Managing writing time: the heart and soul of the writing workshop

- Managing conferring: making one-to-one conferences and small-group instruction possible

- Managing the share session: workshop closure

MANAGING THE MINILESSON: THE BEGINNING OF EACH DAY'S WRITING INSTRUCTION
Convening the Class for the Minilesson

Your writing workshop might begin with students coming in from another class, in which case you'll meet them at the door and make sure they enter and get right to your meeting area, whatever that may be. If you have block scheduling, your workshop might mark a transition from a subject you taught in the same classroom—perhaps your students will have just wrapped up book clubs in reading workshop, in which case you'll need to give a signal that their time for reading is coming to a close, and writing workshop will begin soon. The workshop itself begins when you make it clear that writers need to convene. It is remarkably important for you to develop a consistent ritual for this so that you eliminate transition time. If some students need to move, and/or slightly move some furniture, teach them to do this quickly and quietly, just as they would later in life in a professional meeting.

Experienced workshop teachers are apt to start the year by demonstrating—acting out—their hopes for how students will gather for minilessons. Elisa Zonana does a quick "dry run" or rehearsal with adolescents. Then she sends them back to do it again, and gives them feedback first. "I like the way some of you were pushing in your chairs so others could get by," she says. "I like the way you were making room for others, and saying excuse me." "I like the way a few of you not only brought your own materials, you reminded your partner to do so." The first time I saw Elisa do this, I thought, "What classroom were you just in? I didn't see or hear any of that!" But Elisa has a plan. She role-plays her students into behaviors she wants to instill. In their second run through, you see students doing those things she just praised. In five minutes, Elisa teaches kids what it looks like to be efficient and responsible.

And your goal is just that—that kids act in responsible and mature ways. You're not looking for obedience, you're looking for independence. So make expectations clear, and give feedback. Don't get into a rut where you are constantly giving the same directions. "Come to the meeting area" should soon be code for "Get your stuff, find your partner, find your spot, help shift anything that needs shifting, and do it fast, politely, and well." When kids take forever to move from one part of the room to the other, be clear—that doesn't bode well for them. There aren't a lot of great jobs for people who can't get their act together. Adults convene all the time in high-level jobs, and

they do it fast so they can get to real work. "I'd hire you," is a high accolade for a highly efficient class.

Some teachers use a countdown as a scaffold to move students expeditiously along in the beginning. "Let's take the count of five to gather for a writing minilesson. Five: Look at the way you are getting your notebooks and finding your folders!" Then your countdown can continue. "Four: You are making sure you have something to write with! Three: I notice that you are pushing your chairs in and coming quickly! Two: I see you made sure your partner was all set with everything he or she needs. One: You are opening your notebooks so you are ready to take notes." Of course, before long this behavior becomes automatic, and you need only say, "Join me," and kids make their way to their spots, open their writer's notebooks to the first available page, and look at you.

You may question this detailed attention to how students move from one place to another, and there certainly are teachers who prefer a more organic, easygoing approach. But for lots of teachers, especially those in crowded classrooms, transitions can be a source of delay and tension, and neither is advisable. A fiction writer once said, "The hardest part of writing fiction is getting characters from here to there," and this can be true for teaching as well.

"Make expectations clear, and give feedback. Don't get into a rut where you are constantly giving the same directions."

If you want students' attention but don't need them to gather—like for a mid-workshop teaching point—you can use the attention-getting device again. Most teachers simply stand in a certain part of the room and say, "Writers," with a commanding voice, or "Eyes on me, writers." After saying that (or whatever you choose as your signal) give the classroom a 360° survey, waiting for absolute silence and for all eyes to be on you before proceeding. The important thing is that you use the signal you settle on consistently and teach students to honor it. Don't yell across the room. Do notice individual delays, so you can coach these kids privately later.

Some teachers are uncomfortable insisting on utter silence, and therefore they speak over kids who are still talking. Every now and then you'll have a student with an IEP (Individualized Education Program) who struggles with social cues or is, for whatever reason, a mutterer. Make accommodations for specific behaviors—and overall, insist that your students act in the manner that will make them successful outside your classroom as well as in. If you regularly repeat yourself several times to be sure kids take in what you've said, you are enabling your students to live as if they have comprehension or behavioral problems. The first step to remedying this is to develop a way to signal for students' attention, and the second step is to resist repeating yourself. The third step is to work with kids individually to support their ability to pay attention.

I find it striking that in classrooms in which the transitions are long and mired in tension, teachers often assume this is par for the course. They shrug and say, "What are you going to do?" as if they assume this is how writing workshops proceed in most classrooms. I've come to realize that many aspects of classroom management are shaped more by our teaching—and specifically our expectations—than by our kids' cultural expectations or developmental levels. When teachers make a point of teaching classroom management, thirty kids can come and go quite seamlessly between the meeting area and their workspaces. If they can't manage this simple task, it's hard to imagine what will go well for them. Go study the baseball coach or the basketball coach to see how he or she gets kids moving quickly. Be clear, insist on efficiency, get to work.

Establishing Partnerships

My message is this: help students get into partnerships immediately and immediately give them time to work together. It is quite simple, really. When kids convene for the lesson, have them sit beside a partner, and when they disperse to work independently, have them sit near that partner.

Partners do not write collaboratively, but they function as audiences for each other's writing in progress and frequently make suggestions to each other. Usually partnerships last across an entire unit of study—sometimes longer. Writing partnerships are not tutoring sessions, where one student functions as the "teacher" and the other the "student." These are two people who can work together to help each other raise the level of their writing. You might consider various types of partnerships, and help students move in and out of them. Leveled partnerships are ones where students write more or less at the same level, and/or show the same focus and drive as writers. These types of partnerships let you come alongside more struggling writers and support them, with hints that will be useful to both of them. Often, a strong writer needs to be with another strong writer to really forge ahead. Some teachers will decide that for a particular unit of study, it makes sense to try friendship-based partnership;

teaching friends to push each other academically is a great gift to students. In general in middle school, you will often want kids to feel like they have a hand in choosing their partnerships, while really, you are negotiating them. Gradually, either over the year or across grades, your goal will be for students to seek, work on, and monitor partnerships.

As mentioned earlier, in many classrooms, teachers designate Partner 1 and Partner 2. The advantage of doing this is that during any particular minilesson, chances are good that only one member of each partnership will have time to share, which means that if kids are left on their own, the dominant partner will end up talking all the time and thus receiving all the help. When you've named some partners as Partner 1 and others as Partner 2, you can alternate who does the talking or the reading aloud during limited periods of time.

When particular partnerships work well, you'll want to try to keep them in place over time. It's a great thing in life to find someone who can help you with your writing. If students are English language learners, the partnerships or maybe triads often contain a more and a less proficient speaker of English. For new arrivals, the partnerships may be language-based—two speakers of Urdu working together, for example. You may find yourself with one student whose IEP makes social interactions difficult, or who struggles to work well as a writing partner. Writing workshop doesn't solve the issue of the outlier. Move that student through a series of triads, and/or set that student up to work individually as you help him or her work on social skills. *Don't* become that student's writing partner. All your students will need you to be coaching into partnerships. You'll listen in and give tips as they talk to each other, you'll look over their shoulders and assess, and you'll need to notice trouble and highlight exemplars.

Management during the Minilesson

The biggest challenge you will encounter when teaching a minilesson is achieving that magical balance wherein your kids are wide-awake, active participants—and yet their involvement does not turn a tight, economical bit of explicit instruction into a free-for-all, with chitchat and commentary and questions and free associations overwhelming lines of thought. Over the years, my colleagues and I have recommended different ways for you to walk this delicate balance, and frankly, you'll need to do some self-assessment to decide on a plan that works for you and your students.

For years, we suggested that the best way to keep minilessons streamlined was for you to essentially convey to kids, "For ten minutes at the start of most writing workshops, I'll convene you here for the minilesson and I'll teach you a strategy that you can use to make your writing better. For most of the minilesson, this is my time to talk and your time to listen. I'll tell you what I want to teach and show you how to do it. Then you will have time to talk to a partner as you try what I've taught."

I still believe that many teachers would be wise to convey that message and to teach minilessons in which students are essentially seen and not heard until midway into the minilesson. I say this not because I think it is the perfect solution, but because I think the perfect solution is hard for mortal men and women to achieve. It is a real trick to allow for more active involvement while still modulating—constraining—that involvement so that you protect the work time kids need.

But in this series, we go for the gold. We send a more nuanced message to students. We say to teens, "I'll often channel you to talk—and then before you finish talking, I'll ask you to hold that thought and to listen up while I make a quick point. This means you need to watch my signals. Later in life, you will pay attention to cues in a meeting. There will be times to talk to the group, times to talk with a partner, times to talk to yourself silently, and times to listen."

Thus the minilessons in this series offer many more ways for students to be actively involved in the frontal teaching than they were in the earlier units of study books. I'll summarize the ways we involve students, equip you with some tips for constraining that involvement, and explain our decision making around this.

- One of the goals of the first portion of a minilesson—the *connection*—is to involve students. More specifically, in the connection we often aim to help students recall the prior teaching that provides a context for today's teaching. We are likely, therefore, to ask a question such as "What have you already learned about . . . ?" and to set kids up to talk briefly to their partner about this. Then we pause these conversations, saying, "I heard you saying . . ." and use that as a way to highlight what students already know about a topic. This little activity is varied in a host of ways. We might read off a list of what we have taught, asking students to point to places in their drafts where they did that work—if they did. All of these little interludes for participation can be perceived, by kids, as invitations to tell

the whole class about whatever is on their mind—which then sidetracks the minilesson. So you'll want to ensure that invitations to talk are kept brief and to the point and that you channel students to talk to each other (probably within partnerships) early in the minilesson, and not for half a dozen of them to take the floor, talking to the whole group in ways that slow down the minilesson.

- During the *teaching* portion of a minilesson, we often teach by the method called *demonstration*. We do something in front of the class so young writers can notice how we do that activity—differently than they would probably do it—with the hope that they can come to insights from watching us. The challenge is to demonstrate something that adolescent students can also imagine themselves doing so that as they watch us, they notice how we do things differently—better—in ways that inform their practices. To recruit students to be engaged in our demonstration, we are apt to get students started trying to do the same thing that we will soon demonstrate. We start the demonstration with some guided practice. "How would you do this?" we ask, and get kids started doing the work in their minds. Then—just when they are beginning to do something—we say, "Watch me for a sec." That is what it means to demonstrate. For our performance to function as a demonstration, the learner needs to be about to do the same thing, and ready to notice how we do things differently. This requires a keen level of engagement by the learner, but again, this requires that we recruit kids to be on the edge of doing something, or performing something, and then, instead, we take the lead, pointing out what we hope they notice in our demonstration.

- During the *active engagement* portion of a minilesson, students' engagement of course increases. After demonstrating, the teacher then says, "Now you try this out," or something to that effect, to signify that this is the active engagement section of the minilesson. Teachers set kids up to be fully engaged during this time; usually this means either to "write-in-the-air" or "turn and talk" with a partner. For example, if the minilesson centers on how writers sometimes prop up the author of a source when citing text evidence to add to the overall authority of an argument, the teacher would probably demonstrate by reading a few sentences of a draft in front of the class, pausing when she finds a place where she introduced text evidence, and adding in phrases such as "noted ecologist . . ." or "experts such as so-and-so agree." Then she'd say to the class, "So let's try it." She might set the class up to continue rereading the text, saying, "If you find a place where I included text evidence but didn't do much to prop up the source or make it seem important, would you write-in-the-air, showing your partner how you'd revise my draft?" thereby channeling kids to say aloud the word they recommend substituting. Alternatively, the teacher could ask students to notice and then discuss in pairs the steps she went through to make sources seem more authoritative and significant. "What steps did you see me taking when I replaced *according to the article* with *according to noted oceanographer Jacques Cousteau . . .* ? Turn and talk with your partner."

There are some messages you will want to send kids about your expectations during the minilesson. Students need to know what to do if a partner is absent (join a nearby partnership, perhaps one you've designated as an ambassador partnership, without asking you to problem solve). They need to know that during a minilesson, their job is to listen and look unless you signal for them to do something different—to talk to a partner, to write-in-the-air, to do some fast-writing, to list across their fingers. They probably need to know that there will be times when you ask for students to just say their thoughts into the air, into the group, but that generally, if you are talking, you don't expect them to call out. If that is a message you want to convey—and I suggest you probably do—then be careful not only to say that explicitly to your students but also to hold to it. That means that even if a student calls out something brilliant during the minilesson, you'll want to signal that, actually, this is not a time for kids to say whatever thought crosses their mind. Of course, there will be times for students to talk in a minilesson—often to their partners—so you will want to show them how to make a fast transition from facing forward and listening to facing their partner and talking. They can't spend five minutes getting themselves off the starting block for a turn-and-talk (or a stop-and-jot), because the entire interval of that interlude usually lasts no more than three minutes!

All of these things are worth explicitly teaching. I've watched teachers practice the transition from listening to talking to a partner by saying, "You want to get good at gathering your ideas quickly, talking in intense, low voices, and then listening to a partner—*and* looking to see when it's time to reconvene. So let's try it right now. What's your favorite all-time movie and why? Turn and talk." And then, after a minute, saying, "Back to me." If you take just a minute or two to coach into the behaviors you want and then remember to hold to those expectations later, you'll find this all pays off in giant ways, not just in your classroom, but in your kids' overall social, academic, and professional success in other endeavors.

MANAGING WRITING TIME: THE HEART AND SOUL OF THE WRITING WORKSHOP

While the minilesson sets the tone for the writing workshop and provides students with another teaching point to add to their repertoire of writing strategies, the main work of the day happens during writing time, when students are bent intently over their work, hands flying down the page or over their keyboards, or are alternating between writing something, rereading it, drawing a line, and trying that again, then again. It is during writing time that you are free to support, scaffold, and foster students' growth as writers in whatever ways seem most important for each individual writer. In this section, I'll provide an overview of the structures to consider so that your students are not distracted during writing time, including how to effectively send them off to write, the nature of their work, and how to teach and organize for a collaborative work environment. I'll also talk about ways you can use table compliments and strategy sessions to make your presence felt, and ways you can support students' writing stamina.

Sending Students Off to Work: The Transition from Minilesson to Work Time

Just as you explicitly teach kids how to convene for a minilesson, you will also teach them how to disperse after the minilesson and get started on their work. Students need to learn how to go from the minilesson to their workspaces and then to open up their folders, notebooks, or laptops, decide what they are going to do, *and get started doing it*. If you don't teach them otherwise, some kids will sit idly by until you make your way to that table and give that student a personalized jump start. It's worthwhile to come right out and teach kids how to get themselves started writing. Sometimes you will disperse one cluster of writers at a time. While one cluster goes off to work, you may say to those still sitting in the meeting area, "Let's admire them as they get started right away!" Sometimes you will speak in a stage whisper. "Oh, look, Toni has her notebook open and is rereading the entry she wrote yesterday. That's so smart! I wonder if the others will do that? Oh, look. Jose has gotten out the mentor text and is working with it!" This reminds both the dispersing and the observing kids what you hope they will do. Donna Santman, a master middle school educator, often explicitly tell kids what it should look like if they are being successful. "Here's what it should look like," she'll clarify.

Sometimes you will find it helpful to ask partners first to envision what each will do that day. "Picture the work you want to accomplish today. Quick, tell your partner your plan, so you can check in later to see how it went. Sometimes you disperse kids by saying, "If you are going to be doing [one kind of work], get going. If you are going to be doing [another kind of work], get going. If you are not certain what to do today and need some help, stay here and I'll work with you or set you up with the tools you need."

Other times you will say, "Get started doing that right here in the meeting area," and then you'll watch to see when a student is engaged in the work, tapping that student on the shoulder and gesturing to say, "Go to your work spot and keep writing." Again, this allows you to end with a group in the meeting area who need some help.

Transitions are smoother if kids always know where they'll sit during writing time. You will probably give your students assigned writing spots or negotiate these with them. You'll want to avoid, however, making it a habit to not only tell kids where to sit but to also tell them what to do. This may surprise you. You may think, Doesn't the teacher tell students what to do during the minilesson? Isn't that really the role of the minilesson?

Those are very important questions, and it is true that in traditional instruction, the teacher would use the whole-class instruction at the start of the lesson as the time to show everyone what he or she is expected to do that day. In traditional teaching, during the whole-class instruction, the teacher would assign the day's work, perhaps demonstrate it, and then kids would keep doing that exact same thing across class. But during a workshop, your whole-class instruction aims to add to students' repertoire, teaching them how to do strategies that they will then draw on over and over as they write. So you generally end your minilesson by saying, "So let's review your options for what work you'll do today," or "So when you are ready to work on . . . remember this tip . . . But you can also draw on all you've learned to do, prior to now." That is, fairly often after the minilesson, students will need to reflect on their progress, consider their goals, review their draft, and plan how they'll proceed.

Some students aren't accustomed to making choices about their writing work, and they'll show this by waiting, as if paralyzed, for you to tell them what to do. In a classroom in which kids tend to wait for individual jump starts, I suggest teachers forcefully get themselves out of the role of making individual work plans for writers. It can help to just say to kids, "At the start of each day's writing workshop, I won't be available for conferences. Instead, this is a time for you to make some decisions on your own and for me to admire, research, and record the ways you get yourselves started in your writing."

Leaving kids to make their own decisions will be most challenging if they are in the revision phase of writing. You'll want to specifically reach each of them with how to make wise decisions—but what you'll find you have to do is set them up with overall approaches, and then watch them for how independent they are. For example, I usually tell young writers that if they are not sure what to do as a writer, the wisest course of action is to reread recent writing and think, "What does this piece need me to do next?" I also suggest that if they are stymied, they can look at anchor charts and exemplars for strategies that writers often use and decide which of those strategies might work at that point for their particular piece. Alternatively, they can review their goals, and set to work trying to achieve them. In some classrooms, kids are expected to give themselves an assignment (also referred to as a *planning box*) each day. "Decide what you are going to do, record your plans in a self-assignment box in your notebook, and get started!" Call on role models whom your kids admire—anyone who has risen to prominence in any field has done it through self-direction and hard work. You might say, "Justin Timberlake and Shaun White don't wait for a teacher to appear to say, 'You can start now,' and you don't need to wait for that either."

The Students' Work during the Workshop

The rule during a writing workshop is that during writing time, everyone writes. So there is no such thing as being "done." If a writer completes one thing, then he or she begins the next thing. On a given day, a writer might progress through a sequence of writing work. For example, a writer might study a few exemplar leads, try writing a few leads of his own, select one, and start a draft. This means, of course, that the decision making that I described earlier is something that writers engage in throughout the writing time, and it means that throughout the writing time, you'll want to be ready to support your students in being metacognitive, strategic writers.

You should expect that as your writers progress along through their sequence of work, many of them will come to places where they feel stymied. "I'm stuck," they will say. Or they won't say anything, but they've stopped working. If you set aside some time to do your own writing, you'll find that you also come to a place where you say, "I'm stuck." This is entirely normal for writers.

When kids feel stuck, their first instinct is usually to find the teacher and ask, "What should I do next?" You will want to approach those interactions being clear that your job can't be to dole out all the little steps that every writer is to take. A big part of writing is assessing one's own work, identifying challenges, reviewing possible strategies for responding to those challenges, trying one, assessing how that effort works, and so on. You will not want to remove that entire responsibility from your students' shoulders by allowing them to make you decider-in-chief. Make it clear that you aren't there when it's time for them to work on writing outside of school. You won't go to high school with them, or take the SATs with them, or write that scholarship application. That's why you're setting them up to make increasingly knowledgeable choices as writers.

In minilessons, you can teach them what they can do when they feel stuck—or when they are done or when they don't know how to start writing or when they don't know how to revise. Almost always, you'll respond to these requests for assistance by either turning students back onto their own resources or by teaching them to assess and to identify goals, and by teaching them several possible strategies they might draw on to reach those goals. That instruction can occur in a conference or in small-group work. Both are described in more detail in Chapter 8. In *Choice Words*, Peter Johnston advises that teachers cultivate a language of independence versus a language of obedience or codependence. When a student says he or she *needs* something, he advises you respond, "What are your thoughts on that?" or "Do you need my help or can you figure that out yourself?" Save your instruction for high-leverage teaching, which you'll accomplish in conferences and small groups.

For now, however, let me add that it does help if you have a rough plan in mind for how you hope students are progressing through the writing process, and you share those expectations regularly. If, for example, you are teaching sixth-graders during the literary essay-writing unit, you will want to approach your teaching with a pretty clear sense of the approximate path you expect writers to take. If your intention is for writers to take a little more than a week researching, planning, drafting, and revising one well-developed essay, you will probably want your students to collect entries for a while—more than one entry a day, for two or three days. Then you may expect students to take a day to draft and revise thesis statements as well as plans for the essay. Then you'll expect writers to work for a day to write the essay, and a day or two to revise it. If you enter a unit with a fairly clear sense of the progression that you expect students will experience as they work toward the piece of writing, you can avoid doing things such as teaching students so many good ideas that they never get off the starting block. Be sure that the progression allows for enough writing—your middle school students should be able to write a few pages within a day's writing workshop and a similar amount at home.

Of course, even when a unit is built around clear expectations for student work and student progress, things won't go exactly as planned. You and your students will need to use your best judgment, making decisions about what their pieces of writing need and letting the pieces of writing and the writers' own hopes come together in individualized work plans.

Teaching and Organizing So that Writers Rely on Each Other

There are a few reasons to teach your students to rely on each other. One is that, as we've noted, they will be going on to high school and college with their peers, not with you. So it will serve them well to learn to help each other. Another reason is that they are more available to each other than you can ever be. You simply can't be a partner to each of them. Finally, in the end, your writers will often work on writing tasks alone, and so they need to learn to teach themselves, which they do by engaging in teaching each other.

When you find yourself facing a slew of raised hands, therefore, or notice that kids are standing, waiting for you, you might say, "Writers, can I stop all of you? Would you look at all the people following me! I feel like a pied piper. Writers, today I want to teach you that there is not just one writing teacher in this classroom. Each one of you can be a writing teacher. And you need to become writing teachers for each other because you will be each other's study partners outside of school, and also because this is how we learn to become writing teachers for ourselves—in the end, every writer needs to be his or her own writing teacher. So, right now, let me teach you what writing teachers do for each other. Then those of you in this line behind me can help each other."

Of course, it is helpful for you to think about exactly what it is that you think kids in your particular class *can* do for each other. At a minimum, writers can listen to each other rehearse their subjects, so that may be the first thing you want to coach writers to do for each other. The first step in helping writers do this is to teach them to ask open-ended questions. Demonstrate by having the class help you. "Your job is to ask me questions that get me to talk at length about my subject. Ask questions that get me teaching you about the aspects of my subject that are important to me. Let's try it. I'll be a writer. 'I'm stuck. I don't have much to say. I wrote about Iqbal as a student activist but he was killed by the time he was thirteen, so I don't have much to say.' Remember, your job is to ask me questions to get me talking."

One kid might ask, "Was he murdered?" This is a closed question, and because you want students to ask open-ended questions, you might answer curtly, "Yes." Your hope is that if you do not reward the question with a rich response, the student might glean something about closed questions.

"Was he important?" Again, the question doesn't call for an expansive answer, so you might simply bark out a "Yes."

Eventually, a student will ask a more open-ended question: "Why was Iqbal important?" Respond in a dramatically different way. "Oh! I'm glad you asked. I learned that Iqbal was an escaped student slave. His father had sold him when he was four, and he was chained to a loom. He's important because when he escaped, he became a spokesperson—he went around the world, speaking out about how kids are sold into labor and getting people to not buy carpets made by student slaves. That's why he was killed." Kids probably will have missed what you just tried to demonstrate (yes, it's frustrating), so you'll come right out and name what you've done. "Do you see, writers, that Jeremy asked the kind of question that got me really talking? He didn't ask a yes-or-no question. Instead, he asked, 'What's important about your topic and why?' That's so helpful, because now I have ideas for what to write. And he could help me get even more ideas if he asked follow-up questions. Try it, Jeremy. Ask me to be more specific."

Middle school students can also be taught to help each other plan their writing. They can ask each other questions such as, "How will you start your writing? Have you thought about how you'll let readers know the way your writing is structured? What might you say so they know?"

Students not only need to be taught to help each other in peer conferences, but they also need a structure that allows them to do this. In some classrooms, kids shift between writing and conferring as needed, and this can be workable. Sometimes, however, if kids have standing permission to shift between writing and conferring, very little writing is accomplished, in which case you might wisely insist that writers work silently, conferring only in specified areas of the classroom. For example, some teachers set two pairs of chairs up along the margins of the room; as long as two chairs in the "conference alley" are open, a writer and his or her partner can decide to meet for a five-minute conference (some teachers keep a timer in the conference areas to enforce this time constraint; others add the timer only if the length of conferences becomes a problem).

In addition to student-initiated conversations, you will often ask the whole class to meet with their partners to discuss something specific. Often these partner conversations follow a mid-workshop teaching point or come at the end of a writing workshop. Most writing workshops are punctuated midway through by the teacher standing up in the middle of the workshop hubbub, signaling for attention, and then giving a pointer. For example, "Most of you are having your character talk; in other words, you are including dialogue in your story. Today I want to remind you that writers make sure that the dialogue they include plays an important role in the narrative—demonstrating characters' emotions, for instance, or revealing issues at the heart of your story. Get with your partner and read your quoted sections aloud to each other. Ask, 'Does this dialogue do any work in the story? What does it accomplish?'" A mid-workshop teaching point like this sets partnerships up to talk with each other briefly about a writing technique. Similarly, at the end of the writing workshop, teachers often ask partners to share with each other. "Find a place where your dialogue does some important work in the narrative, and read that aloud to your partner. Then look together at what you've done and name what your dialogue accomplished." Of course, sometimes these interactions are more open-ended: "Writers, would you tell your partner what you did today to meet the goals you set for yourself?" or "With your partner, will you compare the writing you did today with the on-demand assessment piece you wrote two weeks ago and help each other make sure your writing is getting a lot better?"

Using Table Conferences and Strategy Lessons to Keep the Class Productive as a Whole

During a writing workshop, you will alternate between leading small-group work and conducting brief conferences. The small groups will be especially important on days when everyone seems to need some direction. If, for example, you have just taught sixth-graders that essayists elaborate on their thesis statements by making two or three parallel claims, each becoming the topic sentence in a support paragraph, you can anticipate that a third (or even half) of the class will need hands-on help translating your instructions into actions. With such a large-scale need for help, you will probably decide to conduct "table conferences." Instead of gathering selected students together, you can go from one table to another, ask for the attention of all the writers at that table, and then confer with one writer who needs help while the others watch. Of course, the others will not want to watch unless you shift back and forth between conferring with the one student in a way you suspect will help others as well and debriefing. Do this work in a manner that helps not only the focal student but all the others who need similar help: "Do you see how Anthony just did such-and-so? Try doing the same thing right now." Then, as the students begin emulating Anthony's first step, I can help Anthony proceed to another step, one that the observing writers see with only peripheral vision. Soon I'll point out to the table full of listeners that they, too, can do the work Anthony has just done.

I often conduct table conferences during the first few days of the writing workshop and again at the start of each unit of study. At these times, there is a reasonable chance that writers are all at the same place in their work, which is less likely in the middle of a unit of study.

Another way to reach lots of writers efficiently is to sort them into need-based groups and to gather each group for a brief strategy lesson. Again, I describe the methods and content of these lessons elsewhere; for now, the important thing is that you can easily lead four small-group strategy lessons in a single day. These are not formal events. Usually you convene the first group based on the student work examined the night before. Toward the end of the minilesson, I am apt to call out a list of names and say, "Will these writers come work with me after the minilesson?" Then I talk to this group. "I looked over your writing last night and I want to make a suggestion to all of you." I might show this group how they can get past their impasse and ask them to try what I suggested or demonstrated while they continue sitting together. As these writers get started, I might move around the room, ascertaining what others need. If I notice, for example, one writer who is writing without any internal punctuation, I might say to myself out loud, "I wonder if there are others like this student?" Finding others with similar problems, I might gather this group. "I've been looking over your writing, and I have one thing I want to teach you and to ask you to do." While this second group gets started, I might return to the first group. I might check in with each member of the group quickly, then say, "Can I stop you?" and make a point or two that pertains to them all. Alternatively, I might decide to confer with one student while the others watch, making sure I pause periodically to extrapolate larger points from this one situation.

Sometimes, instead of setting out to lead small-group work, you will intend to conduct one-to-one conferences but then you may discover midway through the workshop that you need to reach more writers more efficiently. Therefore, on the spot you shift into leading a small-group strategy lesson or two. You are wise to shift to small-group instruction when you find you are essentially holding the same conference over and over. For example, if I have just helped one student who is writing headings and subheadings for his report to do so in ways that not only take into account the main ideas he wants to communicate but also engage the reader, and then the very next student I approach needs the same kind of help, I am apt to say, "Will you wait for just one second?" while I peer over kids' shoulders to see which other writers may need the same help. Signaling, "Come with me," I soon have six kids pulled into a tight circle in the meeting area or at a table. Often I will then proceed to confer with the first student, only now I do this in a way that makes a point to the larger group.

Then, too, if I am trying to confer and can't because I am swamped with kids who *all* need attention, I may triage these needy writers and work with them in small groups. To one group, I'll say, "I called you together because it seems all of you are having a hard time getting much down on your page. We've been writing for twenty minutes today, and every one of you has less than a page. So let me tell you ways that I get myself to write more, and then let's try those ways, because during writing time, writers need to write. One thing I do a lot when I'm having a hard time writing is thus-and-so."

To another group, I might say, "I called you together because although you are writing up a storm, and that's great, you are forgetting that writers try to use what they know about conventions as they zoom down the page. I don't want you to go to the opposite extreme and spend twenty minutes looking every word up, but I do want you to become accustomed to pausing for just a second as you write to ask, 'Did I spell that word right?' If you need to, you should be using spelling resources as you write." I can also convene kids who spend too long in their peer conferences, who never seem to light upon topics they care about, who forget their writer's notebook, who summarize rather than story-tell in their narratives, who let dialogue swamp their stories, or who need to add transitions to their essays.

Supporting Students' Writing Stamina

What if kids can't sustain work the whole time? Generally, writing workshops consist of ten minutes for a minilesson, thirty, or ideally forty, minutes for writing, small groups and conferring (a few minutes for mid-workshop teaching), and five minutes for a culminating share session. At the start of the year, students who are new to the writing workshop may not be able to sustain writing for thirty or forty minutes. If students are not accustomed to writing for this length of time, after fifteen minutes the class will become restless. A steady rhythm of mid-workshop teaching points that perhaps allow for students to talk with a partner for a few minutes and that also give them a break from the physical act of writing can tide writers over so they can work for longer than would otherwise be possible.

If you see that even after your students have been in a writing workshop for a few weeks, they are still not producing even a page a day during writing time, then you'll want to intervene to increase the volume of writing they do. Start by talking up the fact that writers, like runners, set goals for themselves and then ask kids to push themselves to write more. Then during the workshop, go around cheerleading kids to write more. Make stars or checks on their pages when they produce a certain amount of text. Watch for when a student is pausing too much, and whisper, "Get going!" Midway through the workshop, intervene to ask kids to show with a thumbs up or thumbs down whether they've produced the amount of text you're championing. Use share sessions as a time to count how many lines of text each writer produced. Solicit kids who have increased their volume to talk about what they did to reach this goal. Make charts of "Strategies for Writing More."

Eventually, if some kids aren't getting enough writing done during writing time, ask them to return to their writing at another time of the day—maybe before or after school. Say, "You wouldn't want days to go by without getting

a chance to write at least a page and a half," or "Writers do this. Writers set goals for themselves. Sometimes it does take them a while to get the words on the page, but that's okay. They just rearrange their day so that somehow they get the chance to write." You'll find that the amount of writing your kids do can be transformed in short order if you go after this goal with tenacity, and the same is true for almost any goal you take on!

MANAGING CONFERRING: MAKING ONE-TO-ONE CONFERENCES AND SMALL-GROUP INSTRUCTION POSSIBLE

When you confer and lead small groups, you will probably find it works best to move among students, talking with them at their workplaces, dotting the room with your presence. Although you won't come close to reaching every student every day, you want kids to feel visible. You can hold individual conferences with three kids a day (four or five minutes per conference) and also lead two small groups (they don't require more time than a one-to-one conference), and this will allow you to be a presence in every section of the room. You make your presence matter more because, when talking with one student, you can encourage nearby students to listen in. For most of a conference, you'll probably want to deliberately ignore those listeners, looking intently into the face of the one kid, which often spurs the listeners to eavesdrop all the more intently. Often, as your conference ends, you will want to generalize it to the others who've listened in. "Do any of the rest of you want to try that too?" you might ask. "Great! Do it! I can't wait to see." In Chapter 8, I talk about the internal structure or pattern of conferences and small groups and outline strategies that will help with classroom management. Here I describe conference management practices that help lead students to independence.

Choosing Whom to Confer with or to Include in Small-Group Instruction

Although the context for your conferences and small-group sessions will be created by the entire fabric of your teaching, conferring itself creates its own organizational challenges. For example, you will need to decide how you'll figure out which student to meet with next and which kids to pull together for a small-group session. Teachers develop their own idiosyncratic systems here. Some teachers enter a writing workshop with a little list in hand of writers they plan to see each day. The list may come from studying conferring/small-group records and noticing the students they haven't conferred with for a while, and from thinking about previous conferences that need follow-up. Alternatively, the list may come from thinking about or reading through on-demand writing or current drafts, and deciding on both kids who need help and students who are ready to do more. Have in mind those who could, with help, do exemplary work that might fuel the next minilesson, mid-workshop teaching, or share.

Personally, although I do enter a workshop with a list of the kids with whom I hope to confer, I also find it is important to be able to improvise based on the signals kids give me. So, if kids at one table seem unsettled, I'm apt to confer with a student at that table, knowing that my presence can channel the entire group to work rather than socialize. Then, too, if one student is especially persistent about needing help, I generally assume he needs to be a priority—unless he is always at my elbow, in which case I'll respond differently.

I sometimes tell kids that if they need my help, they should get out of their seats and follow me as I confer, or move to a conferring table and wait until I'm ready for them. I find this keeps the student who feels stymied from derailing his or her companions as well; in addition, the students learn from eavesdropping on conferences. If kids are on their feet, the line that forms behind me also provides me with a very tangible reminder of how many kids feel confused or stuck at any moment, and this keeps me on my toes. If I see more than a few at the conference table, I know I need to get to them or teach them to help each other more.

Keeping Conference Records

You will definitely want to record your conferences and small-group work, and it is important to develop a system for doing so that fits intimately into the rhythms of your own teaching. The important thing is that this record of your teaching must help you teach better and help your students learn better. This writing needs to be attuned to your teaching, reflecting, and planning. You will probably go through a sequence of systems before settling, temporarily, on one. Five or six systems are especially common among the teachers with whom I work.

A lot of our middle school teachers keep digital records, often using Notability or Evernote. These apps let you take quick pictures of student work with your iPhone or iPad, insert that into the note you keep running on that student, jot down your notes, and if you want, share these with kids or parents.

Some teachers keep a page on a clipboard that looks like a month at-a-glance calendar but is, instead, the class-at-a-glance. For the period of time this page represents (which tends to be two weeks) the teacher records the compliment and teaching point of any conference she holds. Sometimes the grid has light lines dividing each student's square into several parallel slots, with alternate slots labeled either *c* or *tp*.

Alternatively, some teachers create a record-keeping sheet that culls some main goals from the learning progression for the type of writing they're teaching, and use it to remind themselves of their goals for students' learning as well as to record their observations of kids' work and their teaching. Some teachers use learning progressions and unit plans to create a prewritten list of possible compliments or teaching points and carry these prewritten teaching points with them, checking off what a student is doing that merits a compliment, what they will teach, and what they recognize they could, but won't be, teaching now.

Some teachers have notebooks (paper or digital) divided into sections, one for each student, and record their conferences and small-group instruction with each student there. Others do a variation of this, recording the conferences and small-group sessions on large printer labels and later sticking the label to the appropriate section of their notebook.

I like to record conferences in a final section of students' writer's notebooks, the logic being that this way when I return for another conference, I can look at both the conference notes and the work. At the same time, the student has a very tangible record of the agreed-on work and the pointers I have made, and this is alongside the student's own goals for him- or herself.

Middle school teachers regularly teach between fifty and one hundred writers. It's too much to expect your working memory to remember every detail of what each student is working on. Develop a record-keeping system and keep innovating it. Talk with colleagues, ask at conferences, keep at it. Digital tools are making this work easier every day.

MANAGING THE SHARE SESSION AND HOMEWORK: WORKSHOP CLOSURE

The title of this time—"the share"—is misleading because actually, this is yet one more opportunity for instruction. In fact, when thinking about the teaching that you'll do on any given day, it is important for you to keep in mind that you'll usually communicate a teaching point in your share as well as in your minilesson. Sometimes that teaching point will bookend the point you made in the minilesson. For example, if your minilesson highlighted the way writers use dialogue to bring a narrative to life, your share might teach students ways to punctuate dialogue. Then again, that same day's share could also provide a counterbalance to the minilesson, perhaps by suggesting that not only do writers stretch out parts of their stories by adding dialogue, they also condense other parts by summarizing.

You will want to induct students into rituals that make the share time efficient. Decide whether you will pull students together for this interlude or not—the choice is yours. If you decide to do so, decide on how you will communicate that writing time is over and it is time to convene. Will a student circle the classroom, letting others know it is almost time for the class to stop work? Will you be the one to convey this message, perhaps saying to the writers, "Three more minutes"? In any case, writers will need a bit of time to finish what they are writing.

Whether you gather students in the meeting area or not, you'll probably begin the share by talking with kids for a minute or two. You may share the efforts of one student, either by reading aloud the earlier and later draft of the student's work or by asking the student to do so. Then, typically, you'll engineer the share so that each student has a chance to talk with his or her partner. For example, you might say, "Did you do similar work? Take a second and reread your latest draft, putting your finger on a spot where you did something similar." Then, after a few minutes and lots of eyeballing, you might say, "Show your partner what you've found."

The discussion of the work students have done during that day's work time will lead naturally into a discussion of their homework. In middle school, it's crucial to be crystal clear about expectations for homework. By high school, kids will do almost all of their serious writing outside of school—they need to bring their work to school, ready to discuss. That means you will want to coach middle school students toward that independence. Often, students' homework will involve doing again whatever the work was that they did in class. "Tonight, your job is to write another part of your literary essay, working carefully to select text evidence, to lead into that evidence and to explain it." Sometimes you'll offer choices—but you should remember that you can offer choices and still be crystal clear about what students are expected to accomplish. "Tonight, your homework is to write between one and a half and two pages. You might do that by continuing with the scene you started today. You might write a new one. Or you might go back and find a scene you want to extend and revise. Ask your partner, 'What choice makes the most sense for you? What will ensure you get that much writing done?'"

If some students do the homework and others do not, this only widens the achievement gap between those who tend to work hard and those tend to slack off. Although it is not easy to influence how students spend their time outside of class, it is important for you to do all you can to rally students to do the work that will enable them to learn. It will help, for starters, if expectations are crystal clear for homework, as are consequences for not doing the homework. It will certainly be important to follow up on homework. It helps to even do something as small as asking students to hold up their homework in class. You can even have them reread their homework at the start of the minilesson, as part of the connection, putting a finger under the place where they did whatever it was you may have set them up to practice. Then, too, make the actual assignment specific. Students can revise however they want, but they need to generate at least a page and a half of new content.

Chapter 7

Inside the Minilesson

JUST AS THE ART INSTRUCTOR pulls students together to learn a new glaze or a new way to mix paints, and the football coach huddles his team to go over a new play, so too do teachers of writing pull kids together for minilessons that open each day's writing workshop. This might mean your students come to a corner of the room that is set up as a gathering place, or it might mean the students in the back move forward to some benches, a carpet, stools, or simply to sit on desks. Gathering for the lesson helps demarcate the part of workshop that is the lesson, from the part where you send kids off to work. So even if it is a symbolic convening with only a few kids moving forward, you want to mark that it's time to convene, and then that it's time to go work.

Minilessons are meant as intervals for explicit, brief instruction in skills and strategies that then become part of a writer's ongoing repertoire, to be drawn on as needed. That is, every day in a writing workshop you gather your writers and say, "I've been thinking about the work you are doing, and I want to give you just one tip, one technique that I think will help with challenges some of you are having or may have soon." Then you demonstrate the new technique and help kids get a bit of assisted practice trying the technique in miniature ways, all within a ten-minute minilesson. After this, you send writers off to continue their important work, reminding them that they can draw on the strategy they learned that day as well as those they've learned previously. I've often said that the most important words of any workshop are those that come at the end, when you say, "Off you go." In any workshop, it is important that the students know how to do just that. They need to know that after the minilesson is over, they can resume the important work they were doing the day before, drawing on all they have learned all year long and especially over the recent weeks and days. Sometimes you'll want to clarify those choices at the end of the minilesson, making sure that each writer has a clear plan for how to accomplish a lot of writing that day.

Usually for a minilesson, kids sit alongside a writing partner, clustered as close to you as possible. This is not a time for kids to sit in a circle, where they can see and interact well with each other, because conversations among the whole class are minimal. This is the time instead for you to teach as efficiently and explicitly as possible. So most teachers decide to ask their students to sit alongside a partner, as close to the teacher and the teaching tools as possible.

Although the teachers with whom I teach often worry over the content of their minilessons, the truth is that if you are teaching and learning alongside a classroom full of students who are engaged in their own writing, you'll soon find that your mind will brim with ideas for minilessons, and of course, you have the minilessons in these units of study to lean on as well. The biggest challenge is learning not the *content* of minilessons but honing your *methods*. Because time in middle schools is always limited, it's extra important that your methods let you teach with the greatest possible efficiency, clarity, and impact.

THE ARCHITECTURE OF A MINILESSON

While the content of minilessons changes from day to day, the architecture of minilessons remains largely the same, and it remains consistent whether you are teaching reading or writing. The architecture of a minilesson (as we have taken to calling the design of a minilesson) is easy to learn and provides support for any minilesson you might ever write.

Minilessons are only ten minutes long, yet within those fleeting minutes there are four component parts:

- Connection
- Teaching
- Active Engagement
- Link

Connection

Minilessons begin with a connection. This is the "listen up" phase of a minilesson. Although this is a whole-class instruction, when taught well, a minilesson has an intimacy, and that feeling is established in the connection. The start of the connnection is a time to draw students in. You might do this by conveying that you've been thinking hard about the content of this minilesson:

- "Come close. I've been thinking about what the one, most important tip I can give you might be, and it is this."
- "Writers, I was studying your writing last night, and there's a particular technique that I think you're ready for . . ."
- "Writers, I have a confession to make. I've never found it easy to (do the work you've been doing). I decided I should let you in on a trick that I've used a lot to help me . . ."

Often the start of the connection is a time to nestle today's instruction into the context of students' prior learning. This may involve finding a way to get students thinking about what they have already learned about a topic—whether that learning occurred during the previous few days or within an earlier unit of study. For example, if you will be teaching students a new technique for editing, you might want them to review the editing checklist they've been using prior to now, noting whether there are some things on it that are second nature to them by now and don't even need to be included in a list of reminders. If you are teaching students ways to end a literary essay, you may remind students of techniques they have been using to end other kinds of writing. The larger context is important because at the end of the minilesson, when you send students off to write, you'll want them to draw on this entire repertoire and not just on the specific technique highlighted today.

In the final part of the connection, you tell students the crux of the minilesson. You do this by giving them your teaching point. Almost always, you signal that students need to listen carefully because you preface the teaching point by the words, "Today I want to teach you . . ." Then you name the teaching point that crystallizes the most important lesson that the minilesson aims to teach. When the minilesson is completed, the teaching point often becomes a new bullet on an anchor chart, and students are reminded that they will want to draw on not just the day's teaching point but also on the larger repertoire of related strategies. Kids then leave the minilesson with not just a single strategy in hand, but rather with an expanded repertoire.

Let's look more closely at both parts of the connection, starting with the first part, where you try to connect today's teaching to the larger canvas of your teaching (and to the kids personally). Over the years, I've developed a few techniques that I tend to rely on.

In the connection, I often try to recruit students to recall the work that they have done prior to this lesson, which provides the context for the lesson.

If I'm going to teach students a new way to write persuasively, I'm apt to start the minilesson by helping kids recall what they already know about argument writing. I might, for example, say to them, "You've learned so much about argument writing. I'm going to reread our anchor chart, and after I read an item, will you give a thumbs up if this is something that you do in your writing and a thumbs down if this isn't something you've tried yet." Then I read the list of techniques for writing arguments that I hope kids are already using and let them know that today they'll have another opportunity to use all the techniques they've already learned—and they'll learn a new technique as well.

There are lots of ways to adapt this general idea. For example, I might say to kids, "I was thinking today about all the ways you've already learned to write arguments. Right now, will you list across your fingers three techniques you use often when you want to take a position and defend it—really argue that position?" Then after a moment for silent thought, I might say, "Turn and talk. What techniques have you already learned for defending a position?" As kids share their techniques, I would probably scrawl what I heard them saying into a list, and then pause the conversations to say, "I heard many of you saying these things," as I then read the list.

I could also draw out students' relevant prior knowledge by saying, "Writers, you're going to be drafting your first chapter of your information book today. I've got one last tip to teach you. Before I add one more thing to your list of all that you already know how to do, will you scan our anchor chart with your partner and notice which of these things you're going to have to keep in mind, and which are just automatic to you by now."

There are more creative ways to accomplish essentially the same thing. "Writers, I don't usually eavesdrop as I walk down the halls, but the other day, two kids were arguing and I couldn't help it, I just had to listen. Let me tell you what they said, because to me, it seemed the argument moves they were making are exactly the same ones we've been learning! Listen, noticing their argument moves. This first eighth-grader said . . ." Then, after telling about the argument and asking students to note the moves the arguers had used, I could list moves I'd noticed as well, and use that as a way to review what the class had learned about argument.

In the connection, I sometimes share tiny excerpts of student work and vignettes from working with students.

I'm always playing up students' work in class, finding one student who does something that can nourish other writers' imaginations of what's possible. But I also keep a file of work from previous years and, frankly, from other people's classes. Kids are interested in other kids even if I need to preface my story by saying, "I'm going to tell you about something that one of last year's seventh-graders did." I save work that is funny, in particular, and also work that represents problems many writers encounter. For example, when I have wanted to teach students that some comparisons are more effective than others, I have told the story of a kid who wanted to describe the sound that the waves make at his beloved beach. The student closed his eyes, re-created the sound in his imagination, and then told me what he planned to write, "The waves sound like a toilet being flushed." I used the story to explore connotations, suggesting the comparison didn't work all that well. When I use an example, I recite the exact words that the student said to me, though I feel free to embellish to make a more engaging story. Minilessons are much better if we tell stories well.

Notice that oftentimes the work I share is not perfect work. In minilessons, I often want to talk to the class about an issue they're tackling, so it helps to tell a little story about a writer who faced similar challenges—that writer might be me, or another kid, or just "writers in general." If the story is being told as a cautionary tale about what *not* to do, I don't use the names and stories of writers in that class, but instead, either put myself in the position of needing to get better at something, or use an example of another young writer whom they don't know.

In the connection, I sometimes try to draw students in by showing them that the upcoming teaching will be relevant to them.

Frankly, sometimes my goal in the connection is simply to secure students' attention. One of the cardinal rules for doing so involves using surprise to draw in readers. For example, I sometimes mention a TV show because I know this will say to students, "Listen up." This is one such connection: "Writers, I have to admit, one of my favorite shows is *Pretty Little Liars*. I was thinking about your writing when I was watching the show last night, because I noticed how the writers of mystery shows like that have to build up to the exciting parts. They don't just drop a scary moment into the middle of a story—instead they build up to the scary part. It reminded me of the work you are all doing in your fiction pieces, the way you are building up to that trouble, that problem that your character will face."

In the connection, I sometimes tell a story that may at first seem to have nothing to do with writing, but in the end, becomes a metaphor for the lesson I need to teach.

I recently told a story to kids about a phone call to my mother. I told them, "She had all these problems that she told me about, and I listened and tried to help. We were in the middle of talking when all of a sudden she said, 'I'm going,' and then bam! She hung up! I was holding a dead phone. I thought, 'Where's my thank you and good-bye?'"

The kids, listening, were entertained because they generally like to hear little true-life vignettes, but they thought the story was unrelated to writing until suddenly, in the teaching point, I made clear the fact that readers, like people talking on the phone, expect a reasonable ending to a story, or to any piece of writing. This, of course, leads right into teaching a variety of ways that writers provide closure to a piece of writing.

In the connection, I sometimes make direct reference to the homework that students should have completed the night before.

In the connection, I often refer to students' homework and get them referring to it as well. Take for example the connection in Session 3 of the sixth-grade unit *Personal Narrative: Crafting Powerful Life Stories*:

> Let's take a minute to share with your partner how you continued to make those important decisions for last night's homework. Open up your notebook to the fast and furious writing you did at home yesterday. Remind your partner of the goal you set for yourself, at the end of the last workshop, and then share how you went about generating your personal narrative topic.

Or Session 4 of the seventh-grade unit *The Art of Argument: Research-Based Essays*:

Writers, I asked you to come with your citations and your reference page. Will you show your partner what you consider to be an especially tricky citation, and explain how you made sure to give credit to your source? When your partner is sharing with you, it is your job to look back and forth between the 'Guidelines for Source Citations and References' chart I gave you yesterday and your partner's work to make sure your partner has given credit responsibly.

Connections like these help to contextualize the teaching point to come, and also help students understand the relevance of their work at home.

The connection ends with a clear teaching point.

The *teaching point* is the last part of the connection. In the teaching point, you'll crystallize what it is you will teach in that day's minilesson. I work hard to make teaching points crystal clear and, when possible, memorable and worth remembering. Listen to a few teaching points.

- "Today I want to remind you that when a writer writes essays—personal, literary, argument, or otherwise—the writer often organizes her opinion and reasons into a boxes-and-bullets structure."

- "Writers, today I want to teach you that when information writers revise, they often consider ways they can add more, or elaborate. Information writers can learn to elaborate by studying mentor texts, taking note of all the different kinds of information that writers use to teach readers about subtopics."

- "Today I want to teach you that writers vary the pace of a story for a reason. Writers elaborate on particular parts of a story to make readers slow down and pay attention to those specific scenes. One strategy that works is to figure out which parts of the story you want to slow down because you are revealing an issue or theme that is at the heart of your story, or you want the reader to learn a lot about the character. Often writers slow down the narrative by elaborating on the character's inner thinking, or by developing details about the setting, including its atsmosphere as well as physical details."

- "Today, I want to remind you that writers, especially writers of information texts, take time to think over the structure for their writing. The structure that a writer anticipates using eventually for a piece of writing becomes the structure that the writer wants to use earlier for research, because that way notes are structured in ways that help them write the report they envision."

- "Today, I want to teach you that when writers build an argument, they start by weighing the reasons and evidence offered up by both sides, remaining open, and suspending judgment so as to develop a considered opinion. And even that opinion, that position, is a preliminary one."

As you study those examples of teaching points and the scores of others in the series, you'll no doubt see that generally, an effective teaching point conveys:

- What writers often try to do—the goal
- Ways writers can go about doing that—the procedure

Very often, the teaching point starts with a phrase or a sentence about a goal that a writer might take on, and then the teaching point conveys the procedure the writer might go through to accomplish that goal. Notice, for example, the third teaching point on the previous page states, "Today I want to teach you that writers vary the pace of a story for a reason. Writers elaborate on particular parts of a story to make readers slow down and pay attention to those specific scenes." That's the goal. It's followed by the way to do this: "One strategy that works is to figure out which parts of the story you want to slow down because you are revealing an issue or theme that is at the heart of your story, or you want the reader to learn a lot about the character. Often writers slow down the narrative by conveying a series of actions that develop the issue or theme, by elaborating on the character's inner thinking, or by developing details about the setting, including its atmosphere as well as its physical details." That's the strategy.

I would not feel as if my teaching point earned its keep if it went like this: "Today I am going to teach you to slow down some parts of the story." It is especially important for teachers to guard against the teaching point being, in actuality, a one-day assignment such as this: "Today I want you to slow

down parts of your story." The implicit assumption there is "Good luck with that. I hope you can figure out how to do it." One way to test whether your teaching point is instructive is to think whether it would be worth posting as a bullet on a chart or reiterating several times within the minilesson. If you wouldn't do either with a teaching point you've written, it probably needs revision. Chances are good if the teaching point is not working, you'll see on second glance that it simply names the terrain that the minilesson will cover or the work that students will do. A strong teaching point crystallizes the most important lessons you hope students learn today and can draw on for the rest of their lives.

Some Cautionary Advice about the Connection in a Minilesson

When watching teachers work with the K–5 *Units of Study in Opinion, Information, and Narrative Writing* series, I find myself wishing I could gather those teachers in a huddle and offer a few tips about minilessons. What I'd want to say to teachers is that we do mean it when we suggest that minilessons should be ten minutes in length. (Okay, sometimes twelve minutes . . .) It will help if you approach a minilesson, knowing that yes, the lesson written in the books can actually be delivered in just about ten minutes. For that to happen, teachers move briskly. If the minilesson suggests that you say, during the connection, "Will you tell each other three things you have learned so far about revision?" and then, as students talk, that you listen in and then call for students' attention, saying, "I heard you say . . . ," know that you actually don't give students time enough to tell each other three things they've learned. They think of those things, they begin talking about them, but by then, you are saying, "I heard you say . . ." And know that actually, you won't have time to continue listening until you have heard a whole collection of wise comments. Listen to a student or two, and then ask for the class's attention. Then, too, you needn't wait for all eyes to be on you before you start saying, "I heard you say that . . ." There are countless little ways to shave minutes off your minilesson, and you absolutely need to do that.

There are several other predictable problems that you will encounter if you attempt to author your own minilessons. Some teachers have been taught

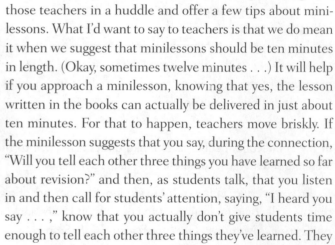

that it is better to elicit information from kids than to say anything to them in a straightforward way. The result is that sometimes the connection to a minilesson is filled with a barrage of questions. "Class, during the last session we talked about . . . what?" the teacher will ask. "And you were having trouble with . . . what?" she'll ask. You will notice in the connections we described that some of them do recruit bits of input from students, but on the whole, in order for minilessons to be only ten minutes long, those bits of involvement need to be very brief. The most valuable place for student participation is later in the minilesson, once you have shown kids how to do something and now want to give them a chance to try that new work out, with support. I suggest, therefore, that you avoid launching minilessons with questions, and, above all, avoid asking known-answer questions in which you're looking for a particular answer. It's just not an effective use of time, and you'll get frustrated because kids can't read your mind, so their answers will tend to take you off in different directions, turning a minilesson into a conversational swamp. You have the floor. Try to speak in interesting and clear ways.

The second problem teachers often have is with grasping the huge difference between teaching a minilesson and giving an assignment. Sometimes teachers will angle their teaching points in ways that sound more like assignments than replicable teaching points. For example, to me if a teacher prefaces what she thinks is a teaching point by saying, "Today I want you to . . ." or "Today you will . . . ," I'm immediately wary that in fact the teacher is not giving a minilesson, but is instead laying out an assignment. A teaching point is a tip that writers can draw on often, whenever they write. So again—be wary of any teaching point that sounds like this: "Today I want you to add dialogue to your story" or "Today I want you to add cross-sectional diagrams to your informational texts." Those are one-time assignments, not teaching points.

How different the message is if you instead say, "Today I want to teach you that whenever you are writing informational texts, it helps if you figure out which ideas and information are best conveyed in words, and which might be better conveyed through diagrams, charts, or other visuals. One way information writers make these decisions is to try out different ways to convey a particular bit of information, then see which method of conveying information seems most appropriate to the content." The difference is not just a matter of words. It's a difference of intent. In a minilesson, you teach writers technique that they can draw on repeatedly, perhaps today, and certainly for the rest of their lives.

Teaching

When planning the teaching, one of the first decisions to make is whether the instruction will rely on a mentor text or not. Often one or two published texts are woven into a unit of study, with students returning to those texts repeatedly to study new dimensions of them. Another option is to look to your own writing. Usually a teacher works his or her way through a piece of writing across the unit of study, in sync with the work the class is doing with its writing. The teacher may actually have completed the piece, but for the sake of instruction, she pretends not to have already written it, rewinding back to the start of the process, so that early in the unit, she might demonstrate how she generates a small list of possible topics and chooses one. Then later, she might show how she gets started writing a first draft, and so on. Sometimes the class also has a text that students have been writing together, and that text, too, might be woven into the minilesson.

While thinking about whether one of those kinds of texts will be brought into the minilesson, you will also want to think about the method of instruction that you will use to teach. As far as I can figure out, there are only four main methods available to us. We can teach people how to do something in the following ways:

- Demonstration

- Guided practice

- Explanation with example

- Inquiry

To help teachers grasp what it means to teach using these four methods, I often ask them to get into pairs, and I then ask one teacher to teach the other how to put on shoes, and to do this bit of instruction using a specific teaching method. (I don't discuss what those methods might be just yet. I simply suggest teachers do this teaching using a specific teaching method.) After two minutes, I stop the group and suggest that now, the second teacher in each partnership teach the first how to put on shoes, only this time I ask the teacher to use a different teaching method. We continue this until people have had four opportunities to teach the one lesson, each time using a different teaching method—how to put on your shoes—and then I ask teachers to list the methods they used. As mentioned earlier, I have come to believe we have only four options: demonstration, guided practice, explanation with example, and inquiry.

Demonstration

The most common way to teach someone how to put on shoes is to begin by first taking off a shoe and proceeding to narrate the step-by-step process of putting the shoe on. That's the method of *demonstration*. The teacher may have done the work previously (I may already have had both my shoes tied securely to my feet when I started this lesson) but the teacher undoes that work (usually behind the scenes) to be able to redo the work publicly, this time naming and then enacting the steps taken and tucking in little pointers. ("Sometimes you need to wiggle your foot from right to left a bit to get it actually into the shoe. Don't step down too hard on the heel of your shoes or it might fold in on you.")

Guided Practice

Second, we can teach in a way that walks our students through the process. Our shoes can stay securely on our feet, and our attention can shift to the learner who needs to start, shoeless. "Okay," we say. "Start by pointing your toe." Then we wait for the sock-footed learner to do that action. "That's it. Now stick that pointed toe right into the shoe, all the way to the far end of it." That's *guided practice*.

During guided practice, we guide students so that they have an instructive experience that they wouldn't have had on their own. We engage students in the activity, and as they proceed, we use clear, efficient prompts to coach them along. We hope that once the minilesson is over, they will be able to do the same processes without requiring our guidance or support. Often once the learner has completed the sequence, we recap the steps taken, using language that makes it likely the learner will be able to apply the teaching to another day, another shoe.

Explanation with Example

We could, instead, give a little lecture, complete with illustrations, to talk through the process of foot insertion into shoe. We could even use Power-Point to make a chart listing the four stages of foot insertion, with pictures to illustrate each stage. That's the method I call *explanation with example*.

The challenge when doing that sort of teaching is to make it informative and memorable. Decide on one name you will give for whatever you are teaching and use that one name four or five times in the minilesson. Think of what you are doing as giving students a little speech on a topic. Ask yourself, "What content can I put in my speech?" Will you share a few tips, tell an anecdote that ends up conveying a lesson, use a metaphor to teach a big idea? You'll want to think over how to make your teaching memorable. Perhaps you'll use an anecdote or a metaphor, parallel construction, or a gesture that represents your content. In any case, this method of teaching requires more (not less) planning than the others.

If your explanation includes showing examples, you need to consider how you'll highlight the aspect that is germane. Often you can bring one aspect into relief by contrasting what will happen against a description of what wouldn't happen.

Inquiry

Then again, we can simply ask, "How do you think I got this shoe on my foot? Here's a shoe, here's a foot. Can you figure it out and name a series of steps?" That's *inquiry*. This method is most common when you want to engage kids in studying an example of good work, or when you want them to contrast effective and ineffective examples, generating descriptors of each. Sometimes this method actually combines the methods of demonstration and guided practice.

Planning a Demonstration: An Example

Each of these methods can be used to teach within a minilesson. To plan how the teaching component will go, I'm going to use the demonstration method as a model, since 80% of our reading and writing minilessons rely on demonstration. Let's say this is my teaching point.

> "Today I want to teach you that when you are hoping to convince someone of your claim, it is important to not only state your claim but also to include reasons. One simple method to accomplish this task is for the writer to state his or her claim, then use *because* to include reasons."

Demonstrate, don't recap.

To devise a minilesson that uses the demonstration method, it's important to guard against simply telling people about something you have already completed. Such a summary might start like this.

"Sixth-graders, I want to tell you that when I was writing my literary essay, arguing that the character Katniss is selfless, I realized I needed to explain my thinking—to add reasons to support my opinion, so I added *because* and then my reasons!"

That's not teaching by demonstration. That's teaching by leaving your shoe on and simply looking back to explain (and perhaps showing an example). In contrast, if I want to demonstrate, the first thing I need to do is to take off my shoe, or to undo the writing work I have already done, so that I can "put my shoe on" (that is, write the passage) in front of the learners. Before proceeding, then, let me share a few other tips about demonstration teaching.

Demonstrate just one strategy, and pick up where you left off writing.

In one minilesson, you do not want to show writers how you choose an issue that matters, decide on an audience, figure out what you're arguing for, and also generate reasons to support that opinion. If the day's minilesson is designed to show writers ways to support their opinion, then the only writing work you will want to do is to generate reasons to support an opinion, perhaps adding those reasons onto your *already-existing* literary essay. So to demonstrate only the new part of your thinking, you need to already have a draft that *doesn't* include any supportive reasons.

Generally in a minilesson—especially one where the teaching method is demonstration—the teacher starts by setting up the context for the minilesson. Often this means showing writers that you have reached a certain spot in your writing process or have encountered some difficulty. Sometimes just slowing yourself down, taking time to think, to struggle, by saying things like "Hmm . . . ," helps. That is, something prompts you to reach out for the strategy you will teach.

"Writers, you'll remember that during the last session we worked together on this literary essay to argue that overall, Katniss, in *The Hunger Games*, is heroic not because she's physically strong but because she's selfless—she's willing to sacrifice herself. In our essay we wrote, 'Katniss has been held up as a modern girl hero, but it's not her physical strength that makes her heroic, it's her willingness to sacrifice herself. Overall, Katniss's dominant trait, the one that makes her heroic, is selflessness.' Now I know that to make a point, writers needs to explain their thinking—they need to add reasons—let's see . . . how could I do that? Let's think about how for a moment . . . I know we want to convince our readers that Katniss is heroic because she's selfless. It's tough, because a lot of readers admire her because she can hunt, and because she's so tough. But we want to show that it's her selflessness that matters. So . . . what reasons can we give? Hmm, . . . It's not always easy to come up with reasons, is it? I have a trick that works for me. Let me show you."

Invite students to imagine doing the demonstration with you.

Brian Cambourne, the great Australian educator, once told me that people fly hang gliders over the field outside his office. On many days, he can look out his office window and see the people strapping themselves into harnesses and running pell-mell toward a cliff, whereupon they launch themselves over the cliff and into the air. Brian pointed out that although he has watched this perhaps several hundred times, those hang gliders aren't functioning as mentors to him because never in a million years would he imagine himself doing what those people are doing. So he watches with detachment, not with intensity as one would in a useful demonstration. In this example, there is a thin line between guiding students to do some work and the teacher demonstrating that work, and that thin line is characteristic of many demonstrations. Often the teacher recruits students to join him in doing something, and then at some point, just when the kids are also engaged in the work, the teacher pulls ahead, performing the work for the students in ways that highlight how he hopes they will all go about doing the work.

Notice that in that demonstration, I said, "What reasons can *we* give?" I acted as if the students are joining me in the work of writing this literary essay, even though in fact this is my demonstration lesson. Here is the important thing. When teaching using the method of demonstration, it is helpful if you talk about the task as if the students are doing it with you, even though (because this is teaching by demonstration), in the end, you will demonstrate in front of them. You might go further by asking kids to join in the demonstration, like this.

"Try this. Try saying our claim and then adding the word *because*. Sometimes reasons come to mind when writers do that. 'We think that Katniss is selfless because . . . A, and also because . . . B.' Let's all see if we can come up with some reasons, okay? 'Katniss is selfless because . . .'"

Then you model. You do the work that you want to show kids how to do. When doing that work, you will want to sometimes mess up in ways that you know kids will also mess up, and then correct yourself, giving you more opportunities to teach. For example, you might say:

"Katniss is selfless because she volunteers to take Prim's place at the reaping . . . no wait, that's really the example of her being selfless, not the reason why I think she is selfless. Let's try again. . . . Katniss is selfless because she voluntarily puts herself in danger in place of others. Okay, that's one reason. Let's try another. . . . Katniss is selfless when she gives Peeta the soup even though she's starving. *No*—that's the example again. So . . . Katniss is selfless because she gives resources she needs to others. Yes, that works."

Debrief what you've demonstrated.

Finally, you will want to explicitly name the steps you took in a way that is replicable to another day and another piece.

"Writers, did you see that to come up with reasons, I said our claim, 'Katniss is selfless . . .' and I added the word *because*, and then I made sure I was saying a reason, not just an example? Sometimes I found myself saying the example and then that led me to the reason. When we wrote those reasons, we made sure to remember that good writing is detailed."

Some cautionary advice about the teaching component of a minilesson.

When coauthoring the middle school series, I had the chance to work extremely closely with a dozen fabulous middle school staff developers and teachers. We planned the teeny tiniest teaching moves together, and studied our teaching plans to make them better, better, and better still. Over the course of that work, I came to understand that the strengths middle school educators bring to this work also set them up for a few predictable challenges. Above all, it is important that you guard against thinking that by performing your own literacy in front of students, your prowess will magically rub off on your students. Watch that you limit the length of your demonstrations—I

generally think there are very few times in minilessons when you need to read or write more than three or four lines of text. Beware against your tendency also to demonstrate by drawing on a magical combination of strategies. Less is more. If you enter a lesson with draft A in hand, and you want to demonstrate B, then the resulting text should be A plus B, without any C, D, or E thrown in!

Active Engagement

After you teach something, you'll want to give kids the opportunity to try what you've taught. Usually you'll do this by involving them in a bit of guided practice in which they do what you've taught while you interject quick prompts that scaffold them through the steps of what you want them to do, or that lift the level of what they are doing. Setting this up takes some doing. Here are some options that are available to you, followed by potential problems to anticipate and solve.

Students continue the work on the next part of the demonstration text.

Sometimes, it works for students to help out with the next bit of work on the demonstration text. For example, in the teaching described earlier, the teacher has demonstrated how to go about adding two reasons to support the opinion, and certainly the most obvious active engagement would be to channel kids to turn and talk, helping each other generate other reasons that could be added. As those kids talk with each other, the teacher might remind them of a few pointers that will make their reasons more convincing, doing this through voiceovers, delivered as they talk in pairs.

Students transfer what they have learned to do to another text—one shared by the class or their own.

Imagine that the minilesson had instead taught students how to title a piece or how to end a piece—or has taught them anything else that one does only once in a piece of writing. In that instance, at the end of the demonstration, the work on that text would be complete! This means that you can't, then, say, "So now your turn. Do what I was doing, only let's progress to the next part of the same text."

In instances in which you are teaching something that happens just once in a text, to set students up to practice, you either need to channel them to try the same work on a shared "exercise text," or you can channel them to try the work on their own writing. To channel students to work on a shared text, you might share a piece of problematic writing with the class and recruit them all to pitch in, suggesting ways to improve that piece of writing. If the teacher is sharing problematic writing, she'll often pretend the text was written by some mystery student or neighbor. "I'm wondering if you guys could help my nephew to do some of that same work. This is what he has written so far. Would you turn and talk? What tips do you have for what he might do next?"

To channel students to try the work on their own writing, you could say, "Would you take a minute and reread your opinion writing from the last session, and will you mark the place where you think you need to add specific reasons?" Then, after a moment of work, the teacher might call out, "Partner 1, tell Partner 2 what you might add. Help each other." You probably will not want students to actually do the work on their own texts, as that will be the work you reserve for them to do during writing time. So you are more apt to suggest they "write-in-the-air" or that they talk about the work they plan to do later. If the work is something that a person does repeatedly, then it is conceivable you might suggest they do one bit of that work during the active engagement, saving the rest for later. For example, if you are helping them to rethink instances when they used adverbs to qualify their verbs, working to instead use a more precise verb, students could try their hand at this work, revising one instance of this during the minilesson, and tackling the others later during the work time.

Students act as researchers, naming what you have done in the demonstration.

Sometimes in the active engagement section of a minilesson, it is challenging to figure out a way for kids to practice what you've just taught quickly, and so you might devise an alternative way for the kids to be actively involved. The easiest alternative to pull off is for you to suggest that kids function as researchers; you'll devise a way for kids to watch someone else (usually you) doing the work, and then you'll ask them to articulate what they observed. You might say, "Tell your partner what you saw me doing that you could do, too,"

or "List three things you saw me do." Sometimes you will want to harvest the students' observations so as to create what can become a helpful chart that can scaffold students as they later go to do this same work. You'll find that if you simply call on students to say into the air some of the things they noticed you doing, the resulting list will be out of sequence and often worded in less than precise ways. You could, of course, work with the class so that is not the case: "Is that the first thing you saw me do? Who can think of something I did before that?" This back-and-forth work is extremely time-consuming and probably not worth the time it requires. A simpler solution is for you to listen in as kids talk with each other, perhaps scrawling onto your clipboard as you listen in. Then you can say, "Class, I heard you say so many important things. I heard you say . . ." and you can read off a list that captures some of what you actually did hear as well as other things you wish you had heard. You might say to the class, "Tonight, I'll write this into a chart so you all can look back on it," allowing you to then produce one chart that can be used by all of your ELA classes. Then again, you may want to make the chart on the spot, that day, in which case as students share observations, you'll probably need to spend less time listening in and more time starting to chart as kids talk to partners. Then when you convene the class to recap what you heard, you can reference the list you just jotted.

> *"You can show students that it is easy to move smoothly from listening, to collaborating with a partner, and then back to listening."*

Predictable problems during the active engagement.

There are a few predictable problems you may encounter during the active engagement phase of a minilesson. First, sometimes students can spend all their time on the logistics and never do the work. This problem can come from teachers not taking the time to preteach the rituals that make active engagement time efficient. For example, students are often asked to work with partners during the active engagement time. If each day, students need to find themselves a partner, working through the social dynamics of that day to sort themselves out, that will require a daily hassle. You will absolutely want to be sure that partners remain across at least a unit of study, and you probably want to ask one person to take the role of Partner 1, the other to be Partner 2, so that you can say, "Partner 1, will you show Partner 2 a place in your draft where you did this and will the two of you work on Partner 1 draft to . . . ?"

Even just the transition from students facing forward, listening to you, to them turning to work with each other can be pretaught. You can show students that it is easy to move smoothly from listening, to collaborating with a partner, and then back to listening. "Watch my partner and me," you can say, roping in a student teacher or another student as your temporary partner. You may want to suggest the "don't do this" alternative as well as the "do this" alternative. You could then reenact some of the inefficiencies you have seen in the class, asking, "Does this look like we're making smart use of our partner time?" Kids will laugh, knowingly. Then, for contrast, you can say, "*Now* watch my partner and me," and this time look your partner in the eyes, nod responsively as he or she talks, move quickly to the next item to try, and so forth.

Although one reason that the active engagement work in a minilesson can be prolonged is that the students haven't been pretaught ways to make these interludes efficient, there are other sources of difficulty as well. First and foremost, you need to keep at the forefront of your mind that things need to move quickly. So if you give directions, make them clear and brief. If a student is confused, wave the others on to do the work while you clarify individually. Don't prolong any portion of this—so instead of explaining what students are to do, then scanning the group to ask "Any questions?" and entertaining one or two, you need to give directions extremely quickly, making today's directions not all that different than yesterday's, and then expect your students to immediately get started doing the work.

You need to be mindful that the work can only take a couple of minutes. That means you can't ask students to reread their entire paper, looking for all the times when they have done one thing or another. Instead, your directions might be, "Glance at the start of your paper and mark one time when you . . ." Then, once a good portion of the class has located an example, carry on. "So now will you turn and talk with your partner . . ." You can't wait until every single student has completed the first step in the sequence of activities before proceeding to the next step! If you wait until each kid has completed the work you channeled them to do, or if you respond to all the confusions and questions that kids have at any point, there will be no time left for the most important part of the workshop!

Link

Writer Donald Murray once told me that the single most important sentence in a paragraph is the last one. "This sentence needs to propel readers onward to the next paragraph," he said. "It needs to be not a closing, but a launch." I remember this advice when I reach the final part in my minilessons. These last few sentences need to encapsulate the content of the minilesson in such a way that kids can carry that content with them as they head off from whole-class, teacher-led work into the whole of their writing lives.

The challenge always when teaching is to make a real difference—a challenge that is not for the faint of heart. It's a tall order indeed to believe that we can call students together, take five or ten minutes to teach a technique, and expect they'll actually add that technique to their repertoire, using it later and even again much later when the time is right. It is crucial to remind kids that the particular teaching point of that day is part of a larger repertoire of strategies that they will be drawing on. This often means that in the link, you will refer to an anchor chart (presumably the same one that was mentioned in the connection). When doing this, you'll want to remind students that the goal is not just to do the work of the day's minilesson, but to draw on what is now an even larger repertoire of strategies. You'll also want to remind them that always, throughout their lives, writers call on a growing repertoire of strategies.

So you'll speak with great energy. "And so I'm hoping that today and every day . . ." you'll say with great solemnity, knowing this repeating phrase may matter more than anything else in your teaching. "Whenever you are in this writing situation, you'll remember you can try . . ."

The link, of course, also needs to channel students to actually accomplish something concrete today, so this might also be a time for brass tacks: what choices they might make that day, which choices make the most sense, what it will look like (sometimes literally how many pages they'll write) if they work efficiently.

Then there is the actual send-off. It might be that you channel those who will be doing one kind of work to get going, then after letting those kids settle themselves down, you might channel those doing a second kind of work to get going. Then again, you might ask every writer to complete something in the meeting area, such as jot a plan, or mark where they will be adding significant revision, and when they have finished, to go back to their work spots.

THE ROLES WRITERS PLAY DURING A MINILESSON

I find it's helpful to teach students what *their* jobs will be in a minilesson. Explicitly. On more than one occasion, you'll say, "Today and every day in the minilesson, when I say, 'Writers, let's convene,' you'll get your writing materials and quickly move to here. Then I'll talk to you for a few minutes. When I talk to you, you're going to *listen*, because I'm going to show you strategies you'll want to use in your writing. You'll do a lot of listening during that first part of the minilesson, no talking." This introduces kids to the connection and the teaching part of a minilesson.

You also want kids to understand the third component, active engagement, and so you'll go on to say, "Then after I show you something I hope will be helpful to you, you'll have time to try the strategy yourself, right here where we're gathered. Usually you'll turn to your partner and do some work together. Sometimes you'll be helping to think about a text the whole class is writing together. Then after the minilesson you'll go off to your writing spots, and you'll carry the strategies with you and use them as you write your own pieces on topics you choose." Your little speech doesn't mean kids now deeply understand what is expected of them during minilessons, but it will help.

You may find yourself worrying over how you'll generate *the content* for your minilessons, and this will be the focus for much of this series. I'm convinced, however, that it's even more important for you to learn *the methods* of leading efficient, effective minilessons. When you study the craft of effective minilessons, this work can change your teaching not only in the writing workshop but also in every discipline, and it can improve not only your whole-class but also your small-group instruction.

Chapter 8

Differentiation
Conferring and Small-Group Work

RESEARCH BY JOHN HATTIE (*Visible Learning*, 2008) and others shows that few things accelerate a learner's progress more than feedback. If learners receive feedback that contains both acknowledgment of what that learner has begun to do that really works and also provides practical next steps toward an ambitious but accessible goal, then learners progress in dramatic ways. This is true whether the student is learning chess or figure skating, statistical calculations, reading, or writing.

When a person is learning to write more effectively, that writing, by its very nature, leaves a physical trail. This means that a teacher can literally hold a learner's progress in her hands. As long as writers keep portfolios or binders or notebooks in which they collect their work over time, whether handwritten or digital, a teacher and a writer can sit side by side and look together at what the writer has done, and at how that work has changed over time, noticing also the extent to which instruction has had traction. Writing *is* visible learning, and this makes feedback to writers all the more potent. Within this series, we structure time for offering feedback and tailoring instruction primarily through conferring and small-group work. In this chapter, I'll lay out:

- ways that teachers find the time for conferring and small-group work
- the architecture of the conference
- the basics of setting up small-group work

FINDING THE TIME FOR CONFERRING AND SMALL-GROUP WORK

Of course, it takes time to read over students' drafts and to hear their thoughts about those drafts, so providing feedback to students' writing is a time-consuming endeavor. In the real world of the middle school day, when kids flock into a room, remain for less than an hour, and then are off to another class, any discussion of perfect conferences or state-of-the-art small-group interactions needs to take into account the restrictions caused by too many students and too little time. Here I'll list and explain some ways that teachers find time for providing feedback and tailoring their teaching.

Teach for Independence

Whenever I gather teachers together to talk to them about the power of one-to-one conferences and small-group instruction, I find that many have trouble listening to a detailed description of what happens within a conference or a small group because their minds are stuck on the questions, "How is any of that possible? How can you give attention to only one student, or only one group of four? What are the others doing?" And if I explain that the others are carrying on, writing with lots of independence, it is not unusual for a teacher to explain to me that the population in her school is not accustomed to or ready for sustaining work without a teacher giving full attention to the work of monitoring the class.

These questions are absolutely critical to the entire enterprise of teaching writing. In fact, I can hardly imagine more important questions. The answers are complicated, and I will try to be as helpful and as clear as I can be. But I also want to suggest that you will benefit more from the upcoming section if you try to let yourself play the believing game. Temporarily set aside the part of you that says, "No way. Not possible." Try reading the upcoming section with an open mind, realizing that in literally thousands and thousands of classrooms, kindergarten through eighth grade, writers can actually carry on as writers with enough independence that teachers can conduct attentive, effective one-to-one conferences and small-group coaching sessions. And those classrooms *are* like yours. The writing workshop is thriving in large cities, in elite private schools, in rural hamlets, in international schools throughout the world, in public schools in Israel and Jordan, Mexico and Sweden—including, in some of those countries, schools that have fifty students in a classroom. The key question is *how* is this done, because there is nothing special in those schools or in those teachers' DNA.

Your students will be most apt to work with enough independence that you are free to teach if they are doing work (or trying to do work) that they can envision doing, want to do, and believe they can do. If your students all seem utterly dependent on you, perhaps you have set the bar too high, for now. If you want to figure out ways to manage the class so that you are freed to teach, you need to provide students with highly motivating, not-too-scary work for them to do. Engaging students in a sequence of steadily more challenging work is a critical part of any good curriculum, so those of you who rely on these units of study should be in good stead. But it is also important for you to always keep in mind that when students appear especially needy, it may be that you've just asked them to take a giant step forward, and they may be signaling to you that they need an interim step.

Then, too, make sure you are clear about what you expect students to do for themselves, and don't give mixed signals. Sometimes a teacher will say to me, "I don't know what to do. My kids keep asking for help with _____." My response is always, "That's because you keep giving them that help." If you consistently say to any student who asks for help, "Your job is to do that as best you can," then they won't find it rewarding to ask you for that kind of help—and they'll stop asking.

If students come to you to ask for anything that is essential to their continued progress, you will want to think about whether you have supported them enough in helping themselves. Is your classroom organized so that only you distribute the stapler? Provide access to the laptops? The bathroom? To a partner who'll listen to a draft? Grant permission to finish one text and start another? If you answer yes to any of those questions, you will need to rethink your systems so that students can carry on independently.

This may make you uneasy. How will you know if the draft has been done well enough that it can be pronounced done? How will you check on the amount of time students spend in a conference if you're not in that loop? The answer, of course, is to actively teach students your expectations, to use the free time you gain to check in on how they have handled the responsibilities you've given them, and to teach in response to what you see. That way, you

> *"Your students will be most apt to work with enough independence that you are free to teach if they are doing work that they can envision doing, want to do, and believe they can do."*

are still able to talk to students about work that has been declared finished and actually didn't match your expectations or about undue time at the printer or in the bathroom. But your interactions will be designed to lift the level of this work not just this one time, but in the future.

When your students come to you hoping for solutions to problems they could have resolved on their own, try to remember that although it may be easy to simply solve the problem, it is wiser to take the time to put yourself out of this job. Ask, "What do you think?" Then add, "So why don't you do that? And next time, I think you could solve a problem like this on your own." Alternatively, you might say, "I'm wondering if you need to come to me. I bet you can figure that out on your own." Your job in the conference will be to help the writer become self-reliant in the future.

This same work can be done in a small group. "I called you guys together because all of you are asking for similar help, so I wanted to talk to you as a group. You're all asking, 'Can I be done?' and I wanted to let you know the sorts of things you can do to answer that question for yourself. The first thing . . ."

As you do this teaching, whether in conferences or in small groups, remember that you help students become more self-reliant by reminding them to draw on the classroom charts that contain all the tips they've been taught all year long.

Designing Doable Systems for Grading Student Work

Teachers need doable systems for grading student work—they need to spend more time teaching and less time grading. (Grading student work is not synonymous with giving feedback, although there is overlap.)

Most teachers believe that a portion of the grade given should reflect the students' abilities to produce work (independently and in short order) that meets expectations. In districts that have adopted the Common Core, those expectations are benchmarked against the standards. Most teachers, then, derive a portion of their students' grades from measuring the extent to which the students' written products approach, meet, or exceed the Common Core standards.

In another book within this series, *Writing Pathways: Performance Assessments and Learning Progressions*, you'll learn about the assessment system that undergirds this series. This system revolves around you giving each of your students at least two rounds of on-demand writing assessments in each of the three modes: narrative, information, and argument writing. The fact

that you will conduct a pre- and postassessment in those three modes allows you to gauge the extent to which a given student's independent writing does or does not meet expectations. The postassessment also allows you to gauge the extent to which your teaching from any given unit stuck.

Most of the teachers we know best use the students' levels of achievement as a portion of their grades, and the improvement in their achievement as another portion. That is, if a student enters her sixth-grade year writing arguments, for example, that are gauged as being at the third-grade level, and she progresses dramatically but remains still below standards, the teacher may decide to give that student points for progress.

You may ask whether the teacher, him- or herself, needs to do all the assessing of on-demand writing. Most teachers *do* take on this job, but some ask their students to arrive at their own levels by self-assessing. Because levels of achievement are based upon the comparisons between a piece of writing and the ladder of exemplar pieces in *Writing Pathways*, and because each of those pieces and levels of writing is also captured in a matching student-friendly CCSS-aligned checklist, it is possible for students themselves to self-assess their writing, with the teacher or a peer providing a confirming (or disconfirming) assessment.

I know you will turn to *Writing Pathways* to learn more about these on-demand writing assessments, but in any case, you will want other sources of input to influence your students' grades.

Most teachers also grade the final products that students produce. Often students just complete one final product after a month of work, so assessing those final publications is not terribly onerous. The grades may contain a breakdown of scores, with one score for the sheer quality of the writing (perhaps in relation to the checklist, described earlier), with a second score reflecting the extent to which students demonstrate a command of whatever the teacher has especially taught, and perhaps a third score reflecting the writer's commitment to the writing process and work throughout the process.

The combination of grades from on-demand writing (both achievement and growth, in the three modes) and grades from students' final publications (both product and process goals) will go a long way toward justifying a report-card grade for each of your students. You can, of course, take other factors into consideration, as long as you make these public. For example, you could calculate into the equation a grade for the sheer volume of writing that each student does, or for the degree of hard work the student exhibits, or for the student's abilities to help other students, or for the student's revisions.

Some teachers are expected to produce a grade each week for each student, so that parents and students can track the ups and downs of their progress. If that's the case, you'll no doubt use the students' on-demand pre-assessment for the grade from one week at the very beginning of the unit, the on-demand postassessment for one of the grades at the end of the unit. The publication will then provide another grade, toward the end of the unit. But midway through the unit, there would be weeks without readily available grades. We suggest you let students know that in those instances, you have a short list of expectations for their writing, and you will select any one of these as a lens for assessing student writing (without telling students which of these you will select). That means that one week, you could glance through all your students' writing, looking exclusively at the sheer volume of work produced, and you could give each student a grade based on that. Another week, you could ask students to Post-it places where they'd done their most extensive revisions, and you could glance over those revisions and grade the depth and extensiveness of them.

Setting Up Structures to Support Peer-Feedback

Middle school students need more feedback than teachers will be able to give, and they thrive on interactions with each other. It is helpful, therefore, if peers are taught to give feedback and equipped with exemplars and checklists to support that process. As students learn to give peer feedback to each other, they learn to give it also to themselves, becoming their own first critics—and freeing up teachers to offer individually tailored instruction to others.

It is impossible to emphasize enough how important it is for middle school students to share their writing with peers, rereading each other's writing, responding to the content and talking with each other about what they were trying to do and how well they pulled off their intentions. Conversations that go back and forth between writers should be filled with sentence starters such as "I like how you . . ." "Where did you get the idea to . . ." "I think the first part of it works, though I am not as sure about the end . . ." "Do you have ideas for what to do next?" "How will you try to make it better?"

Throughout this series, students are always working in partnerships with another writer. Almost every day begins and ends with partners talking together, often in ways that have been influenced by the work of the day and

set into motion by the teacher. If the minilesson has suggested that writers can study mentor texts and learn strategies for elaborating in their own nonfiction writing, you may ask partners to study the mentor text together, making plans for which of the techniques they notice that they'll try in their own writing, and then, at the end of the workshop, you may channel those same partners to show each other the work they actually accomplished.

Because these peer relationships are potentially so critical to writers' growth, you will want to do everything possible to lift the level of them. In part, this will mean teaching partners that it is important to show each other they are truly interested. Leaning in to listen matters, as does asking follow-up questions and leaving spaces for the speaker to say more. Then, too, you'll want to urge partners to think about how to help each other grow. Encourage writers to give each other specific suggestions. Coach partners to listen for the writer's energy and to always keep in mind the cardinal rule: the writer's energy for writing should go up, not down.

Then, too, you'll want to make sure you tap into the power of peer response in ways that go beyond the everyday partnership conversation. Think of it this way. If you are lucky, your school is led by a principal who sees the potential in others, and enables those others to assume some of their own leadership roles. In a really effective writing workshop, teachers act like effective leaders—seeing strengths in students and capitalizing on those strengths. "You should lead a study group on that!" "You should help some of the others who are really struggling with that." If you lead by seeing potential in others and creating structures that allow that potential to be shared, then your classroom will be filled with apprenticeships, with collaboration, with feedback that comes from all sides . . . and with writers who outgrow themselves.

THE ARCHITECTURE OF A CONFERENCE

Once you've set up your teaching to make one-to-one conferring possible, you are ready to make those conferences as effective as they can be. Framing your conferences within a powerful architecture is one way to do that.

Most of us do not realize that there are times when our interactions with others follow a predictable structure, but this is nevertheless the case. In traditional classrooms, for example, the teacher will often ask a question, elicit a response from a student, and then evaluate that response. That is, the teacher asks, "What is the capital of New York?" The student responds, "Albany." The teacher assesses, saying, "Very good." This pattern of interaction doesn't often occur outside of classrooms and is not generally regarded as ideal. Usually, if a person asks, "What is the capital of New York State?" and learns that it is Albany, the response would be "Thanks," not "Very good." Teachers who follow this question-response-evaluation pattern of interaction may not realize they are doing so. They may aim to change their teaching and do so by working with new content (asking questions about Vermont, not New York, or about the transportation, not the government of the state) without realizing that as long as the nature of their interactions remains the same, the most important aspect of their teaching has not changed. The truth of the matter is that as long as the pattern of interaction in these teachers' teaching remains the same, the instruction itself will convey many of the same messages.

When a teacher confers with a writer, her interactions tend to follow a consistent pattern, one that teachers of writing have deliberately chosen and that reflects many beliefs about learning, teaching, and writing development. So, although conferences *appear* to be warm, informal conversations, they are in fact highly principled teaching interactions, carefully designed to move writers along learning pathways. Here, I hope to elucidate the principles that guide me and others as we confer with young writers. Specifically, I'll discuss the architecture of writing conferences. Although writing conferences are intimate, infinitely varied conversations between a learner and a coach, there is a way the structure of one writing conference is very similar to another. Afterward, I'll describe how the architecture of small-group work is very similar to that of a conference.

For any writing conference to work, the writer must first be engaged in writing work. That is, you must first organize and teach the whole class in such a way that each student is engaged in his or her own purposeful work as a writer. Then you observe and coach in ways that either help the learner do what he or she is trying to do or that direct the learner to take on new (and perhaps more challenging) intentions. Either way, once you channel a writer toward more challenging work, you may need to briefly scaffold that new level of work. Then you pull back, encouraging the student to continue without relying on you as much.

This means that a writing conference almost always involves these four phases:

- **Research** what the writer is intending to do and has done.
- **Decide** what to teach and how to teach it.

- **Teach** using one of four methods (demonstration, guided practice, explanation with example, or inquiry), then perhaps provide some guided practice.
- **Link** by extrapolating from today's work whatever it is that the writer will want to carry forward into work on other pieces, other days.

The predictability of these interactions makes them more powerful because writers can, in the end, use this same progression to confer with each other and with themselves. These units of study books are dotted with examples of conferences that follow this architecture. As you read them you will see these principles in action.

The Research Phase

When I help teachers learn to confer well, I focus first on the importance of research, since it is research that allows your conferring to be responsive and accountable in ways that make your teaching responsive and accountable. When you conduct research during a conference, you sit eye-to-eye with the results of your teaching. You confront ways in which your teaching has worked and has not yet worked. You listen to the writer, you look at the page, and you see the power of what you taught or you face the fact that your eloquent minilesson (or ours) didn't do the job. Either way, you think: Now what? And there, in that moment, with you and this student who is relying on you, you invent a new way to teach. You nudge the student to explain what he was thinking, and you listen so you can tap the power of the writer's dawning insights or so you can pinpoint the disconnect. When a conference doesn't begin with a teacher taking into account what the writer has done and is trying to do, then during the teaching phase of the conference, the teacher often just reiterates teaching that has already happened, unaffected by this particular student and his or her work. The vitality, originality, and specificity that characterize powerful conferences require that you, as a teacher, take in what the writer is understanding, doing, planning, and working to achieve.

And then, because you have done this research, you invent new teaching right there on the spot—new teaching that may well find its way into a small group, a mid-workshop teaching point, a share session, a minilesson, a new unit of study. Because you research, you end up creating an exemplar, right on the spot—one you hope will be connected with this student. You use something that just happened in the class as a metaphor. You make teaching that is newly minted, and that works in part because it is just that: responsive, new, tentative, your own. Your conferences become a source of originality and power in your teaching.

This is not always the case. Many teachers don't spend enough time trying to understand what the writer is doing and why, and in conjunction with this, they use conferences as merely time to recap the minilesson and to check that kids are doing whatever he or she channeled writers to do. There are two important problems with this—first, it means the teacher never accesses the power that conferring has to enliven and personalize his or her teaching, and secondly, the teacher's conferences are unnecessarily slow. Why bother researching if there is no real chance that your teaching is going to be newly minted in response to what a writer shows and tells you? Why not just cut to the chase and use that time to teach?

So a discussion on the research component of a conference needs to begin with a frank discussion of the purpose for that research. Know from the start that the reason to engage in research is so that the teaching you do will be responsive. So when you slow yourself down and do the research that I describe in this section, aim for your teaching to be something other than a mere recap of that day's minilesson, or the preceding day's minilesson. You may see that the writer is clearly grasping and doing even more than you taught, in which case, think about how you can you tap that writer's experience and ability to help others. Could you channel the writer to help another student—as doing so would also cement the writer's new knowledge? Could you tell the story of this writer in a small-group session or in a mid-workshop or a share—if so, you will want to be able to tell what the writer did first, then how he or she improved on that. The story will be more effective if there is a beginning, a middle (the strategy, the process), and an end to it. Then again, perhaps the writer only partially understood what you hoped to teach. You'll need to think about another way to explain, demonstrate, scaffold—in short, to teach. The good news is you can try that new teaching out in the safety of this one-to-one conversation, and if it works: presto! You have something to bring to a small group of others who struggle similarly or to the larger group, if the problem feels universal. If all bodes well, a day from now you

will even have some student work to illustrate not only the problem but also the solution!

Before I launch into instruction on how to do this life-giving research, it is important to acknowledge that sometimes you bypass research, or cut it short, on purpose. Kids are misbehaving: having side conversations that are unrelated to the work of a writer, roughhousing, being loud and off task. You needn't look each writer in the eyes and say, "How's it going on? What are you working on as a writer?" You *know* how it's going—not well—and you know full well the writer is not working on much! Then, too, you and a student had a long conference two days ago. Now you just want to check back in. Sure—you need to say, "Let me see what you've done since we talked" so you can be sure the work is on course, but if your aim is simply to give a compliment and to renew the "keep at it" charge, your research will amount to nothing more than a quick check-in.

Your own experience being observed and coached can be a source of insight.

To understand the research part of conferring, think about times when someone has conferred with you. Think, for example, of your principal, talking with you before making a visit to your classroom. My hunch is that you are pleased if the principal asks questions such as, "What have you been working on in your teaching? How's that been going?" "What problems are you running into?" "What feedback could I give that might be helpful?" Questions such as those are helpful in and of themselves because they lead a person to reflect. Even before the observation occurs, then, the process is already helpful, leading to dawning insights, crystallized goals.

Of course, questions such as those can be asked in a manner that makes them utterly unhelpful. Those questions can be helpful or they can lead you to stammer out a robotic answer. The difference revolves around your sense of whether the person was really interested and sympathetic. When a coach really listens, leaning in to hear more, nodding in ways that convey, "Say more," that intense and generous listening leads the learner to say more. A good conference begins with deep listening.

Ask the learner to teach you her intentions, strategies, self-assessments, plans—not about the topic.

The research component of a conference usually begins before you even glance at the writer's paper. You want to understand what the writer has already been doing, so as you approach a writer, you notice the writer's all-important engagement in his writing. You glance at the page, not reading it just yet, but trying to glean any information that can help you learn about the writer's work. Then you ask about the writer's process, intentions, self-assessment, plans, hopes As the writer talks, you may read bits of the writer's work so that you triangulate what you hear with what you see, taking in information from all possible sources, and you may quiet the writer for a second so you can read a bit more.

Be careful of veering into talking about the writer's topic; that conversation would not constitute research. That conversation would be something else—perhaps you have leapt ahead in the components of a conference and you are providing a sort of compliment or teaching (though probably not an effective version of either) or perhaps you are being sociable, talking together as you might talk before class. There are reasons to do this—and sometimes the content of a piece of writing is such that this is exactly what is called for. But know that talking about the topic of the piece, right at the start of a conference (before you have taken in other information), means you have put the research on hold.

So, you start the research by taking in all the information you can and then launching an inquiry. You ask a cluster of related questions to understand what the writer has been doing and thinking. You might ask questions such as these: "When we talked last, you were planning to. . . . Can you fill me in on what you did since then, and what you're thinking about that work?' If this conference doesn't feel like part of a trajectory of work—if the aim instead is to launch such a trajectory, you might ask, "Can you talk to me about this piece you are working on? Would you say it is one of your best pieces, or not such a good one? What parts do you like, what parts don't you like? What could you do if you wanted to make it even better?" Then again, another line of questioning might unfold like this: "What have you been trying to do especially as you write? Can you take me

to a place where you did that? How do you think it works? If you were going to make this even stronger, what might you do?"

Once a writer has told you what she is trying to do, you'll probe to understand what the student means. If the writer says, "Yes, I'm unpacking my evidence," you might say, "Can you show me where you did that?" Or "If you were going to unpack this example, how might you do that?" Of course, you usually have your own understanding of the terms your students use (because they use the very terms you've taught them), but it is crucial to help a student articulate what *she* means by those terms because often it is not the same as what you mean.

You can remind yourself of how important these questions are if you remember that these conferences are not unlike the interactions you have with principals and staff developers who are going to observe your teaching. You want the person who coaches *you* to first listen to learn what you have been trying to do, to learn about your goals—you're doing the same for the people you coach.

Sometimes kids aren't good at answering questions about their writing intentions and strategies—what then?

Let's face it, sometimes you ask all the right questions and kids look at you with blank faces as if they have no clue what you are talking about. Or they answer—but it's the kids, not you, who veer straight into a conversation about the topic rather than the writing process.

"What are you working on as a writer?" you ask. The writer answers "My dog," and launches into a detailed description of the dog. In those instances, the key thing to remember is that you need to explicitly teach students their role in a conference. That means you need to lift a hand up to signal, "Whoa. Stop, stop," and you need to explicitly say, "When I ask, 'What are you working on as a writer?' I'm not wanting you to tell me about content ('your dog') or even your genre and content ('a poem about my dog'), but I'm wanting you to tell me about your goals and strategies ('I'm writing a poem about my dog *and I'm trying to be sure readers can visualize my dog, so I'm adding metaphor, and trying not to mix my metaphor*')."

The key is that you need to explicitly teach kids their roles in a conference. "When I ask, 'What have you been working on as a writer?' I'm wanting to know what new stuff you are trying to do to get to be an even stronger writer. Like, for example, have you been . . . ?" And then you might fill in some of the answers you anticipate the writer producing. "Have you been rereading to see what images will be especially strong so far? Have you been trying your piece one way, then another?"

Students who have not grown up in writing workshops may still find it hard to put their goals and strategies into words, in which case you may need to name what it is that you see the student doing, thereby giving that writer words to articulate her intentions. For example, if the writer is revising an essay, you might say, "I'm noticing that you are revising. It looks like you are trying to make sure that the examples you use are angled so they make the point you want to make. Am I right?"

Make sure to pursue more than one line of questioning in your conference.

One way or another, then, you will get yourself into a conversation about the writer's process, intentions, goals, and so forth. What you will find is that these questions will lead you fairly quickly to a place where the natural next step is to stop asking questions and instead, to teach. Say you asked what the writer was working on, you heard he had been working on his ending, you learned that he doesn't like the ending—and so, at that point, you will feel propelled to teach the writer another way to end the piece.

I suggest you resist the urge to do that.

That is, one of the rules of thumb that I especially emphasize is that once you ask the writer a question about his writing and follow that line of questioning to a place where you have grasped one thing about the writer and his work and are tempted to launch into some teaching about that one point, resist that urge. If you can, suspend closure. Don't settle for a single line of inquiry.

Instead, return to a second line of questioning, following that new inquiry through so that you also understand another aspect of the writer and the work.

At the very least, if you first asked what the writer was working on and learned about his work with the ending of a piece, for example, you might then say, "So one thing you are doing is working on an ending, and to do that you are . . . What are some of the *other* things you plan to do with this piece of writing today?"

Of course, that second question could have been entirely different. If you had been asking about the writer's intentions and process, ask about her evaluation of the piece. If you had been asking about the writer's evaluation,

ask about her work with the mentor text in relation to the piece. Get a second line of inquiry going in part because then you will have yet another possible teaching point looming large, and most of all because the fact that you have drawn on several sources of information means you'll be left with a decision to make: "What, above all, could I teach that would make the biggest possible difference for this writer?"

The Decision Phase

To an outside observer, a conference may seem fairly relaxed. But for me, as a teacher, conferences are anything but. As the writer talks and as my eyes quickly take in notes from previous conferences and the draft and any other available data, my mind is always in high gear. Malcolm Gladwell, the author of the best-selling book *Blink: The Power of Thinking without Thinking* (2007), suggests that he can observe a married couple for just half an hour and predict the chances that their marriage will be intact a decade hence. In a conference, I'm trying to do an equally astonishing feat of "thin-slicing." I take in all the data I can quickly assimilate, and as I do this, I'm theorizing, predicting, connecting this writer to other writers I've known, determining priorities, imagining alternative ways to respond, and lesson planning! All this must happen while I smile genially and allow myself to be captivated enough by what the teen says so as to keep the data coming my way! This is no easy task, and teachers are wise to recognize that this invisible aspect of teaching writing is the most challenging one of all.

The decision phase of a conference runs concurrent with the research, and also involves that moment after the research when you take a deep breath before charging on. In that moment, you'll quickly synthesize what you have learned, thinking especially about the learning pathways that the student is traveling along. For example, a student is somewhere in a learning progression that relates to the type of text she is making. Relative to that, she is somewhere on the journey of learning to structure that kind of text, to elaborate on that kind of text. You need to ascertain where the writer is on that pathway so you can help her progress to the next step. You might say to the writer, "Hmm, . . . You've told me a lot about your process and your writing plans. I need to think for a moment about what the most important coaching I can give you might be." That is, you can deliberately delay acting on what you have learned for a moment while you make a conscious decision. What is it you can teach that will make the biggest impact on this learner's writing—not only in this instance but in her whole life? There is no one right answer to this question, of course. In making this decision, you'll draw on the following considerations.

You want to teach every student to become someone who has intentions for his writing, assesses, sets a course, and acts deliberately.

Given that there is no one right way to improve any piece of writing, you'll want to listen to the writer's self-assessment, the writer's goals and plans, and to either teach within the context of the overall direction the writer has set or to talk to the writer about that overall direction, resetting it. If the writer thinks this is the best piece she has ever written and is working to copy most of it over, making only fine-tuning tweaks, you need to know that before proceeding. You'll either go with the writer's intention and help her pull it off, or you'll need to start by addressing that intention, hoping to alter it altogether. One way or the other, you need to leave a writer with an intention and a strategy, a plan, for implementing the intention.

Teach the writer, not the writing. If you don't want to get behind the writer's existing intentions (or if you can't discern what these are), it is important to rally the writer to take on a new intention with commitment.

Responsive teaching doesn't mean that you simply buy into whatever a writer wants to do. Your teaching will be goal-driven. Your goals will come from your knowledge of the standards toward which you are teaching. It is your job to move students to (and beyond) grade-level expectations. Your goals will come also from your own values and resolutions, but it is also important to you to support students' initiative, zeal, and willingness to take risks and to work hard. These goals need to influence your ways of working in a conference.

If a student is writing in generalizations without any detail at all, you could simply elicit details and get the writer to record them. But that would essentially amount to bypassing the writer to repair the writing. The problem with such an approach is that the writing can get better, but the writer will tend not to learn anything from this that he or she can do another day with another piece. So if the writer is writing without any detail, your first job is to show the writer that this is the case and to help the writer embrace the goal of writing with detail. *Then* you can proceed to show the writer a strategy for eliciting those details and getting them recorded on the page.

Always teach toward growth—and eventual independence.

In the decision phase of a conference, you will be thinking, "What is the most important way I can help this writer become a dramatically better writer?" That is an entirely different question than the one you will be tempted to think about. That is, you must not be asking, "What would I do to improve this draft if the piece was mine?"

As you think about goals, think about big and ambitious trajectories you can channel a writer to pursue, not about little things a writer could do for five minutes to fix up a draft. Aim to help the student make a big step forward. On the other hand, the goal is for the writer to be able to approximate the important work you describe with independence, so balance wanting to challenge the writer with acknowledging that you need to teach what is next on this writer's horizon.

During the decision phase of a conference, you will also decide on *how* you will teach. You'll teach using one (and sometimes more than one) of the four methods described in Chapter 7: demonstration, guided practice, explanation with example, and inquiry.

The Teaching Phase

After you've made a decision about what and how you'll teach, you'll begin teaching. The teaching component of a conference usually (but not always) contains a compliment and a mission, a teaching point.

Of course, people need to earn compliments through hard work. If a writer has slapped something on a page, the last thing you want to do is to invent some trumped-up compliment that doesn't ring true. A conference is a time for eye-to-eye talk. "Frankly, this is what I see, and what I suggest," you say. Hemingway once said, "A good writer needs to have a 100% fool-proof crap detector," and I'd say, "A good writing *teacher* (especially a good middle school writing teacher) needs a 100% fool-proof crap detector."

But it is also the case that some human beings are so constituted that we look at student work, and we see what could still be done, we see next steps. Others look at student work and it looks great. What more is there to do? It is important for us, as teachers, to know ourselves. I tend always to see next steps, so I force myself to make an especially big deal of the compliment part of a conference and try to find aspects to compliment even if they don't immediately meet the eye. You may be the opposite. It may come as second nature to you to name what works in a piece, and you may need to push yourself to imagine big ambitious next steps. In that case, even if a draft looks fine and dandy to you, you'll want to push yourself to remember that even skilled writers deserve to be challenged.

Name an area of writing strength; compliment the writer on a transferable skill or strategy.

When complimenting a writer, you want to name a skill or strategy that the writer is just starting to use and that will be powerful when used often, in many pieces of writing. To settle upon something to compliment then, you need to be able to extrapolate a transferable, generalizable strategy or skill out of the details of the student's work. "I love how you put so much detail into that image of your cousin, rocking the car of the Ferris wheel when it stopped at the very top of the ride. I can see you eyeing the cars below. You wrote with the same kind of detail over here, when you described the particular way your cousin pleaded with you to go on that ride. I think what is really key is that you describe not just what people do, but how they do it, and you use just ordinary interactions to show the kinds of people these are. What you are doing is very writerly—it's a gift you have that you will want to use always when you write narratives." The challenge is to notice a very specific way the writer has succeeded and then to phrase the compliment in such a way that he or she understands how to carry this skill into work on other pieces and other days.

If the writer notes a phrase that a character in a story uses repeatedly—say, the farmhand says, "By God, I will" over and over—you won't say, "I love that you added how Warren says 'By God, I will' repeatedly. I hope you put 'By God, I will' into your all your literary essays!" Instead, you'll name what the writer has done in a way that makes the action replicable: "I love the way you noticed patterns in the text, and brought those into your essay. You always want to remember to do that."

The best is if you can actually take in the new work that a student has tackled and compliment something that represents the outer edge of his or her development. John Hattie's research suggests that compliments—what he refers to as *medals*—need to be informative. The point is not to pile on platitudes. It is to let a writer know that something he or she has been doing is really working—something the writer may not even realize he or she has been doing.

Teach and coach, reducing the scaffolding as you work together.

After complimenting the writer on what he or she is doing that works, you'll want to teach. The teaching phase of a conference is remarkably similar to a minilesson, only it is condensed. First, you'll make it clear that the conference has turned a corner. You might say something like, "There's one tip, one very important tip, that I think will help you not only with this piece but with future pieces. One thing I'd suggest is . . ." Alternatively, you might say, "May I teach you one thing that I think will help you a lot?" One way or another, you will want to signal that you are now instructing the writer in something new that he or she will want to learn.

Then you name what it is you are teaching just as you name a teaching point. In a teaching point, you avoid making this sound like a one-day assignment and instead you word your point so that it is something that writers can add to their repertoire (and their charts) and draw upon repeatedly for years to come. Do the same now. So instead of saying, "One thing I want you to do is to reread this paragraph as if you are a stranger to it and think about the questions you have," you will say, "One thing that writers do after they finish a draft is they sometimes reread their writing, almost pretending they've never seen the piece before, trying to glean what questions the piece will generate." Later, after the writer has tried this, you'll be apt to say, "Did you see the way in which you . . . ?"

In a minilesson, after you name the teaching point you tend to teach the writer how to do that work. You may demonstrate, saying "Watch me do this with the class text." On the other hand, you may decide not to demonstrate, but instead support the writer with guided practice, saying, "Get started doing this and let me coach you in the steps to take. For starters, why don't you . . . ?" As you watch the writer work, however, you may shift out of guided practice

> *"The act of leaving a conference involves taking a second to clarify the work the writer still needs to do."*

and into demonstration, or explain and give an example. For instance, you may pause the writer from doing whatever you are scaffolding, and you may say, "Let me show you the work another writer did, because it could help you."

The Link Phase

The challenge is to do all this quickly—and then to leave. I sometimes suggest teachers confer on their knees, crouching alongside a writer's desk, because the position is so uncomfortable that we rarely overstay our welcome! Always when conferring, you need to be aware of the ticking clock. A conference could take three minutes, or four. It might conceivably take five. But a conference can't be longer than that, ever.

You'll decide when to leave. It may be that you research, decide, compliment, and then name a teaching point—and by then, you see the rest of the room needs you, so you essentially say, "Good luck. I'll check back to see how you do with this." Other times it will be essential to demonstrate and to stay while the writer gets started on the work.

Either way, the act of leaving involves taking a second to clarify the work the writer still needs to do. "I can see you have added a lot of information to the bare-bones passages you had written earlier—here's my thought. Now that you know how to say more, do you think that after this, even when you write new things, you could work to say *more* about each thing? Maybe aim for a page, right from the start, about each subtopic."

Often when you get up to leave a conference, it feels as if the writer is reaching out to grab your shirttails, saying, "Wait, wait, I'm not yet sure. Would it work if I . . ." and all I can say is that you need to know how to leave. "I know you can solve that on your own!" you can say, wriggling out of the learner's grasp. You may say, "That's such a great question. I can't wait to see what you figure out!" You might sympathize. "You are so right to ask. This is a big decision point in your writing. But here's the thing—you are the writer. You are the boss. You make your best decision, and move on—and afterward you can look back and think, 'That worked!' or 'Oops.'"

Although many writers will never feel ready for you to leave, so if you remind the writer that it will be important to continue doing this good work often in future writing pieces, you'll explicitly support transference of what you have taught today into the student's ongoing independent writing process.

The challenge is to do all this, making sure the student's energy for writing goes up, not down. The single most important guideline to keep in mind in a conference is this: the writer should leave wanting to write.

Still, how do you get to everyone?

You don't. Unless you have fewer or smaller classes than most middle school teachers, chances are good that there will be whole stretches of the year when you do not confer with every student. If you were to aim to confer with each student in a dutiful cycle, then you would never get back to any student enough to follow a line of work with that student and to harvest the insights and the materials that can then inform your teaching.

So settle on this. Make sure that during any one chunk of the year, you are conferring with an array of kids who represent the diversity of your classroom, as those students will inform you about not only their work, but also the work of others who are like them. Make sure that you read the work of students you do not actually reach in one-to-one conferences, and either leave them notes or design small groups tailored to what you learn they need from reading their work. Be sure you include lots of ways in which your instruction is reaching all kids—minilessons, checklists, exemplar pieces, small groups, mid-workshop teaching points, instructional shares, peer-to-peer teaching . . . the works. And meanwhile, over the course of a year, alternate the focal kids so that you give that very potent one-to-one attention to each writer for a chunk of time.

Small-Group Work

But meanwhile, a good part of your solution to reaching every student is to teach not only through one-to-one conferences but also through small groups.

How are small groups formed?

The hyper-focus in the United States on record keeping, accountability, and data-based teaching has led U.S. middle school teachers into a tizzy over the topic of small-group instruction. Lots of innovations are being piloted—and a consensus has yet to emerge. Join the exploration!

For now, it is probably safe to say that about half the middle school writing workshop teachers form and disband small groups regularly in a need-based fashion, and the other half form goal-based groups, from students' self-assessments using the checklists for narrative, information, and argument writing (see *Writing Pathways*). Of course, teachers do a bit of both.

One kind of small-group work is the kind that follows directly on the heels of a minilesson. Many teachers regularly end their minilesson by getting students going on the work they plan to do next. There are different ways to do that—perhaps the teacher says, "Get started doing that right now, sitting right here," and then once an individual seems well launched, the teacher says "Off you go" to one, then the next. Alternately, the teacher may say, "How many of you are going to be doing X?" and then when hands go up, she sends those students off, saying, "Get started." She then asks, "How many of you are going to be doing Y?" and again, sends those kids off. Either of these two options results in a group of students remaining in the meeting area, so that the teacher then says, "If you are not sure what exactly to do today, gather around." Then, she can teach those who need a bit more instruction.

There are other ways that teachers fashion small groups at the start of a workshop. She may begin the minilesson by saying, "I studied your work last night and I want to meet with these students after the minilesson." Or she may say, "Would you and your partner (or just you) look over your writing and decide, 'Is my main problem X?' 'Is my main problem Y?'" Then she might say, "Thumbs up, those of you who think you are struggling especially with X," and follow that up with, "Can we meet at the back table at 10:00?"

Other small groups are formed right in the midst of writing time. If you pull in to confer with a student, note what it is that you need to teach the writer, and then if you get a suspicion that actually, there are others needing the same thing, you could say to the writer, "Can I leave you for just a second?" Then you race about the room, gathering up a few other writers who appear to need similar help. Alternatively, you could have just spoken to the class, loudly: "Writers, I'm going to be helping so-and-so with such-and-such, and I'm pretty sure five or six of you need this same help, so come join us."

Of course, if these groups are based on assessments and goal-setting, that means that after the on-demand assessment, you will have recruited students to join you in assessing themselves, asking them to locate and identify their own goals. You will no doubt find that there are about a quarter of your students who need help with structure, another quarter who need help with elaboration, and you can convene these clusters of students. One piece of good news is that you will also have students who are strong in these and other qualities, and they can be tapped as coteachers.

What happens during small-group instruction?

During small-group instruction, the work of phase one and two of conferring (research and decision) has happened prior to pulling the group of writers together. That is, you will have noticed several students struggling with a similar problem—for example, their new drafts resemble the old—and you'll have already decided they would benefit from a small-group session. In this way, the research and decision phases happen on the run and prior to your small-group coaching, and therefore don't need to happen when the group is gathered before you.

Typically you will begin a small group with a teaching point. Usually this starts with you saying, "I gathered you together because . . ." and then you name a shared challenge that the members of the group seem to be facing. Then you say whatever you want to teach, again trying to say this in a way that will pertain not just to today but to future days. "What I want to tell you is that whenever you are stuck in a problem like this, it usually works to . . ."

You might do a very short demonstration, usually working with the class text so that you don't have to take time to introduce students to a new text.

Then comes the important part of small-group instruction—the time when you say, "So right now, get started doing this." Then as students practice the new skill or strategy, you move quickly from student to student, scaffolding with brief voiceover prompts. "That's it—keep going." "Don't forget to cite your sources." Then you move on to watch and coach into the next writer's work. After a few minutes, you convene the writers and explain that the work they have been doing with your support is work you hope they continue to do as they work independently.

Whether you spend most of the workshop conferring or split your time between conferring and small-group coaching sessions, the challenge is to teach effectively and quickly. Once you become skilled at this general template, it will allow you to channel your attention and thoughts to individual writers and to decide on and support the specific next steps each student can take.

It is tremendously important that as you are conferring and working with small groups, you also teach students to confer with themselves. You need to ask writers the questions that they can profitably ask themselves. And you need, as much as possible, to hand over the conferences to the students, letting them become, with your support, both writers and readers, creators and critics.

Chapter 9

Building Your Own
Units of Study

IF THIS SERIES has done its job well it will not only have helped you to teach the units described to good effect, but it also will have encouraged you to work collaboratively with your colleagues to author your own units of study. In their book, *Professional Capital*, Michael Fullan and Andy Hargreaves (2012) point out that master teachers not only study and learn best practices; they also have the skills, the knowledge, and the confidence to develop the next practices. This series has been carefully constructed with an eye toward teaching you to author your own units of study in writing.

In this chapter, I pass along what I've learned about the process of developing curriculum in hope that this can help you and your colleagues create units of study to fill gaps that we have left in the curriculum. You'll want to be in a position to respond to priorities in your region, and to your students' interests as well as your own, by authoring units that aren't described in these Units of Study. The book *If . . . Then . . . Curriculum: Assessment-Based Instruction* will help you imagine some possible alternative and additional units, and I hope some of these units appeal to you so that the chapters in that book can function as a scaffold, supporting you as you develop your own writing curriculum. But I also know that you will want to develop your own units of study from scratch; this chapter can help you do that. I do have some broad principles that I recommend to any school that is developing or adapting a sequence of units in the teaching of writing.

BROAD PRINCIPLES TO KEEP IN MIND AS YOU AUTHOR WRITING CURRICULUM

Consider a Progression of Difficulty

Just as readers learn over time, with practice and instruction, to handle increasingly complex texts, so too, writers, with practice and instruction, can learn to write increasingly complex texts. You will want to study the standards so that you understand the way that expectations grow for writers each year, with students being expected to produce work that stands on the shoulders of the preceding year. For example, when writing argument pieces, sixth-graders are expected to introduce claims and organize their reasons and evidence clearly. By seventh grade, the expectation grows; now, in addition to introducing claims and organizing their reasons and evidence, writers need to acknowledge opposing or alternate claims. You'll need to design your curriculum accordingly.

Plan for Skills to Become Increasingly Automatic

It is usually easier for writers to apply a new writing strategy while in the revision stage of the process. The next time they write something, students should be able to apply that strategy earlier in the writing process since it will not be as challenging or new, and thus can be done with increasing automaticity. What was once a skill or strategy that was applied just before finishing a piece can move to earlier in the process—and instead can become something a writer does during planning or drafting. For example, the adding in of punctuation around quotations might at first be something a student does just before she publishes her work. Eventually, though, with practice, she should be able to include that punctuation in first-draft writing.

Plan for Skills and Strategies to Be Applied over Larger and Larger Spans of Text

In general, it is easier to do something in just a part of a text, and harder to do something across an entire text. For example, in fourth grade, students work to bring out the central idea in each chapter of their information books, but with more experience, by sixth grade they work to bring out the central idea across the whole book. Similarly, it is easier to reread a story and to think about one instance where the character feels something that could be shown rather than told, and it's harder to reread a story and think about making the entire narrative show rather than tell.

Consider that It Is Generally Easiest to Write about What Is Close and Well Known

For most students, is easier to write on topics one knows well, and then progress to topics on which one is more unfamiliar. For example, if you want to teach students to write cross-curricular research-based information writing,

a precursor to the interdisciplinary unit may be one in which students write information books on topics of personal expertise.

Remember that Mastery Does Not Come from Doing Something Once

Students need to be given repeated opportunities to produce a particular kind of writing for them to learn to do that work well enough to meet vigorous standards. For anyone to become highly skilled at a specific type of writing, that person needs opportunities for repeated practice. This means that when planning curriculum, you'll need to plan to provide repeated opportunities for students to engage in a kind of work.

STEPS TOWARD BUILDING A UNIT OF STUDY

As you hold the general principles above for building curriculum in mind, we recommend trying the specific steps below for building your own unit of study.

Although there are as many ways to write curriculum as there are curriculum writers, after authoring and piloting and reauthoring and repiloting literally hundreds of units of study for hundreds of classrooms over the past decade, we've found these steps, in this order, to be the most efficient and generally helpful ones to follow.

Decide on the Subject for Your Unit of Study

First, you will need to decide on what it is you will teach, above all in your unit.

What kind of unit will it be?

You will see that the units that we've detailed in this series tend to be **genre-based**; genre is one of the great organizers of writing. Genre is a rather obvious way to organize students' work with writing. It is easier to imagine planning a unit of study on a kind of writing—whether that writing consists of op-ed columns or research reports—than on a part of the writing process or a quality of good writing, because units on a particular genre will inevitably encompass the full span of the writing process. In a genre study, students begin to imagine what they will be writing by doing some reading. Then they rehearse, draft, revise, and edit that kind of writing—either progressing through one cycle or through many cycles of writing, producing one finished text or many. Certainly there are many genres that have not been addressed in the current series. Some of these—such as historical fiction, poetry, and fantasy—have been sketched out in *If . . . Then . . . Curriculum*, but many others remain as wide-open terrain for your unit writing.

It is also important for you to understand that you can design units of study that are not genre based. Some units are designed based on focusing on one stage in the writing process; they are **process-based**. For example, you could design a unit of study *Revision*, channeling students to review their folders full of writing and to select several pieces from throughout the year that deserve to be revised, then helping them set to work with those pieces of writing. In a similar way, you could conceivably design a unit of study that is **strategy-based**—on a strategy such as using authors as mentors. This, like a unit on revision, could involve students revising pieces they wrote earlier in the year, but this time doing so by studying and emulating the work of published authors. Alternatively, you could develop a unit focusing on a **quality of good writing**, such as showing not telling. In that case, you could rally students to closely study places where authors do that work. Students could then revise their existing writing to show, not tell, in the ways they've learned, and eventually they could draft new texts, applying from the beginning all they've learned. There are other qualities of good writing that could lead to high-intensity and interesting units of study: studying characterization, for example, or the development of tone and voice in argument writing.

Then, too, you could study a **social structure that supports writing**. For example, you could design a unit of study called *Writing Friendships*, in which you help students consider how to work well with a partner and perhaps with a writing club. How might a writing partnership best help with rehearsal for writing? With drafting? With revision?

Although it is possible to design units of study on topics such as these rather than on genre, these topics will be more challenging. If you have experience developing units of study for writing, have a mentor work closely with you, or if you are following one of the plans laid out in the *If . . . Then . . . Curriculum* book, you might decide to try your hand at such a unit. In the absence of these supports, I suggest you may want to start by developing a genre-based unit of study. In any case, take some time to mull over possible topics within writing for the unit, guarding against the temptation to seize on the first topic of study that comes to mind.

Which unit of study would especially benefit your students, keeping in mind what they can do and can almost do?

When you decide on a unit of study, you are taking it on yourself to channel the young people in your care to devote at least a month of their writing lives toward the topic that you settle on. Therefore, it is important to weigh whether a particular topic will be especially beneficial for students. When a unit of study comes to mind, you'll want to put it through the test of asking a few hard questions. Start by asking, "Will the skills students develop during this unit of study be important ones for them? Will the unit be a high-leverage one, setting students up to do similar work in other genres or in other areas of the curriculum?" For example, a teacher decides that she wants her students to become more skilled at writing proficient first-draft writing on demand. For this reason, she may decide to turn the classroom into a newsroom and teach her class to write news articles and editorials. That decision makes sense.

It goes without saying that you need to believe any unit of study that you teach (or any unit you impose on your students) must be incredibly important. You probably won't want to channel all of your students to spend a month or six weeks of time working on a genre that doesn't seem to you as if it will provide them with skills that will be foundational or transferable. For example, a unit on limericks or sea shanties or haiku might be fun, but before embarking on such a unit, I'd want to weigh whether it would pay off as much as other units.

Then, too, think about how the unit relates to your students' skill levels in relation to standards for their grade and to their zone of proximal development. As you think about this, you'll find yourself homing in on what, exactly, you will be teaching within the topic. For example, one could teach a unit on investigative journalism that reminded students of what they already know about the structure of information writing and that focused especially on research—on collecting and integrating information from a wide variety of sources and synthesizing that information into coherent texts. Alternatively, a unit on investigative journalism could help students write what they already know—about events in school, home, and their community—with an emphasis on the essentials of information writing. In the same way, if you were to teach a unit on revision, the decision to address that topic wouldn't, alone, provide a clear direction for your unit. Do you want to focus on students writing to discover new insights or on the physical tools for (and reasons for) adding and subtracting to a text and the challenges of elaboration? Of course, you could select an entirely different focus altogether for a unit on revision. My point only is that once you decide on the terrain for the unit of study you will teach, you still need to home in on specific skills, and to do that, you need to know your students well and to think hard about their entire writing curriculum.

For example, if you and your colleagues decided to develop a unit of study on poetry, you'd want to think about how that unit would fit into earlier and later work across students' school careers on poetry—and on writing in general. You would want to take some time to create a gradient of difficulty for studying poetry. What might be more accessible for your less fluent writers? More demanding for more sophisticated writers? You might, for example, decide that for more novice writers, a unit on poetry could high-light reading-writing connections and revision, and for more proficient writers, a unit on poetry could also highlight imagery and metaphor. Of course, both reading-writing connections and metaphor can be taught in simpler or more complex ways, so you and your colleagues might decide instead to study imagery and metaphor across the grades, with increasing levels of sophistication and challenge.

Here is a final word about one's choice of a unit of study: the other deciding factor is *you*. If you are learning to play the guitar and find yourself dying for the chance to dig into songwriting, then consider bringing that passion into the classroom. If you loved teaching your fiction unit and yearn to do more, consider a unit on revision or on character development (which could invite students to revise several earlier pieces to bring the characters more to life), or historical fiction, or fantasy. In the end, students can grow as writers within any unit of study. And whether you are teaching a unit on indepen-dence in the writing workshop or on writing to change the world, you need to remember in particular that you are teaching students, and teaching writing. The rest is negotiable.

"Students can grow as writers within any unit of study."

Plan the Work Students Will Do

It is tempting to start planning a unit of study by writing a minilesson for Day One and then for Day Two. What I have found is that if I proceed in that manner, chances are great that those intricate, time-consuming first miniles-sons will end up being jettisoned.

I recommend instead that you begin by thinking about the work that you envision your students doing in this unit. For example, before you can imagine the unit's flow, you need to decide whether students will be writing one piece during the unit, or two or many. Assuming they are cycling through the writing process more than once, writing more than one text, will they work the whole time on one kind of writing, or will they start with one kind of writing before switching to another kind? For example, in one unit students begin by writing short observation-based newscasts and end by writing more sophisticated, research-based investigative journalism; in another they begin by writing theme-based literary essays and end by writing comparative literary essays. Also, you need to decide whether writers will proceed in synchronization with one another or whether some students will write three texts and some only one. Then, too, you need to decide whether you imagine students progressing quickly through rehearsal, spending more time on revision, or vice versa.

We always spend a lot of time constructing a storyline through the unit, one that orients the bends in the road of the unit. The storyline for the sixth-grade literary essays, for example, proceeds as follows. Since this is a new genre for students as middle school writers, we begin by putting them all into an intensive shared experience of essay writing. Over the course of a day or two, all students participate in what we refer to as "essay boot camp." During that time, all students fast-write a very quick literary essay that is structured in the simplest, most traditional fashion possible—but is nonetheless structured. Then the next phase of the unit begins. Students learn to live like literary essayists, studying texts and characters, collecting the grist for literary essays, and growing ideas in their writer's notebooks. Those ideas might be written as rough essays, or they may be written as freewriting. Then writers are brought step by step through a detailed process of writing an essay before they are released and encouraged to write another essay, this time a comparative essay, and this time, written while on their own.

When planning the work that students will do, it is important to think about the progression of endeavors that they might possibly take on, choosing work that will be challenging for the class but not so challenging that they are brought to a halt. For example, writing a major investigative piece is daunting, so in the eighth-grade *Investigative Journalism* unit we start students off small, by teaching them how to notice the little dramas happening around them and writing newscasts. Their first piece is to write a "who, what, when, where, why, and how" piece about a staged classroom crisis—a teacher (who has been briefed before) walks in and announces that the State Department of Education won't allow students to read books about romance, and so he must confiscate all the Hunger Games, Divergent, and Mortal Instruments books. Once that teacher leaves the room, the classroom teacher teaches students how to harvest what they witnessed and turn it into a simple newscast. Students have a couple of opportunities to observe small moments in the school setting on the lookout for material for a good newscast, and by the end of Bend I, they will have produced a number of short newscasts.

As students become more proficient, they step up to more sophisticated work. In Bend II, they narrow their focus to a social issue that they care about, learning how to angle their writing to point their readers toward a bigger truth that they want to convey. And so on.

It helps to imagine different ways that the unit of study you've selected might proceed and then weigh the pros and cons of those alternatives. Whatever the genre, whatever the form, there are some principles that underlie the progressions in most units. Early in the unit, students generally work in sync to complete one or sometimes two pieces of writing. During this phase, we do a lot of instruction, and that teaching is captured on anchor charts. Then in most units, we ask students to transfer what they have just learned to the work they do writing a new piece of writing. They work on the new text with new levels of independence, and they not only apply all they've learned during the first portion of the unit, but they also stand on the shoulders of that early work to reach for more demanding goals.

These are a few common templates, then, for a unit of study:

- **TEMPLATE NUMBER 1**
  Your students might generate lots of one kind of writing, perhaps taking each bit of writing through a somewhat limited amount of revision. Then they look back over all of that writing to choose one piece (presumably from the writing they've only lightly revised) to delve into with more depth, bringing it to completion. After this, students work on the entire cycle of writing, this time working under the influence of a mentor text, aiming to do all they did previously, only better now, as they emulate published work.

- **TEMPLATE NUMBER 2**
  Your students may start with an intensive, two-day immersion into the kind of writing they will be doing in the unit, doing this work with lots of support from you. Then all the members of the class work in sync on their own writing projects. This project contains lots of parts or steps, and you coach writers along each step (or aspect) of the piece. After completing that one main project, students fast-draft a quicker version of that project.

Let's imagine that you decide to teach a unit on poetry. You'd probably find this fits best into the first template. Presumably, at the start of the unit each student could write and lightly revise a bunch of poems. Then writers could commit themselves to taking one poem (or a collection of poems that address one topic) through more extensive revision and editing. They could then work through a similar cycle, perhaps this time writing a poetic picture book, not a poem. A unit of study on news articles could fit into that same template. News stories are written quickly, so students could generate many of these at the start of the unit, bringing more and more knowledge to them as they continue to learn more. Then you could explain that sometimes a writer decides to expand the news article into a more developed sort of writing, and you could teach students to rewrite one of their articles as an investigative report or an editorial (either project would require more research and revision).

On the other hand, you might decide that within one unit, students will work on a single, large writing project, say a piece of literary nonfiction, one requiring research. Perhaps for this unit, each student will investigate a different environmental issue. You may decide that the first half of the unit will focus not on drafting information writing but on note-taking. Then, during the second half of the unit, students could draft their literary nonfiction. The unit might end with you teaching writers that the work they do when writing feature articles is not unlike the work of writing literary nonfiction books, and with all students working on a quick cycle to write feature articles.

My larger point is that before I write a single minilesson, I pull out a blank calendar for the unit and plan how the students' work is likely to unfold across the month or six weeks. If I imagine that for the first week or week and a half in a unit, students will gather entries, I mark those days on the calendar. I do not yet know the specific minilessons I will teach, but I do know the broad picture of what they will be doing during those days. Proceeding in a similar fashion, I mark off the bends in the road of a unit. Even after this, however, I'm still not ready to write minilessons.

Gather and Study Texts for Students to Emulate

Before embarking on writing the minilessons in a unit of study, I gather and select between examples of the sort of texts I hope students will write. That is, if you decide to teach a unit on writing editorials and to emphasize the importance of the counterargument, you'll want to turn your classroom library upside down looking for examples of that kind of writing. You'll become a magnet for this sort of writing and find examples of it throughout your life. You may or may not want to invite your students to join you in this search, depending on where they are in their writing and reading lives at the time. Soon you will have gathered a pile of writing, and you can begin to sift and sort through it, thinking:

- What are the different categories of texts here?
- What are the defining features of this sort of writing?
- Which of these texts could become exemplars for the unit of study?

To make these decisions, you'll need to think not only about the texts but also about your kids and about the standards that your school has adopted. You will want to aim toward goals that are achievable for your students, and you will also want to be sure that over the course of the school year, your students meet the standards your school has adopted. For me, this means teaching in ways that are aligned to the Common Core State Standards.

Although I often gather a small stack of relevant texts, I generally select just two or perhaps three to use with students during any one unit of study.

To decide on the texts that you will use as exemplars, you'll need to take into consideration the particular focus you will bring to this unit. For example, when I taught middle school students to write fiction, I knew that I wanted their stories to involve just two or three characters and to take place across just two or three small moments. I knew, also, that I wanted the fiction to be realistic fiction. Fiction comes in all shapes and sizes, so I conduct a thorough search before settling on *Thirteen and a Half*.

Often, you will decide to use your own writing as one of the touchstone texts for the class, and you might also decide to use writing done by another student from another year. These are perfectly reasonable choices. When teaching students to write literary essays, position papers, or research-based argument essays, it is unlikely that you'll find published work closely resembling the work you expect students to produce, so your own writing will become especially important in such instances.

Read, Write, and Study What You Will Teach

I describe units as if they are courses of study for students, but the truth is they are also courses for us! In addition to collecting examples of the sort of writing you'll be asking kids to do, you will also want to scoop up all the professional books and articles you can find pertaining to your unit of study. You can learn a lot from books for adult writers, so don't limit yourself to books by and for teachers.

I cannot stress enough that you also need to do the writing that you are asking your kids to do. You needn't devote a lot of time to this. The writing that you use as an exemplar text needs to be very brief anyhow, so even ten minutes of writing, four times a week, will give you tons of material to bring into your minilessons. The important thing is that during those ten minutes you work in very strategic ways. Usually you'll begin with a bare-bones small text, and you'll develop or revise it in exactly the same ways that you suggest your kids try.

As you read and write, try to think about ways in which the current unit of study could build on previous learning. Not everything that you and your students do in this unit can be brand-new. What is it that students already know that they can call on within this unit? What will the new work be?

Think, also, about what is essential in the unit and what is more detailed work. The answer to that question lies not only in the unit itself but in your hopes for how this unit of study will help your kids develop as writers. If you are teaching poetry with a hope that this will lead students toward being able to engage in much more extensive revision, then this goal influences your decision about what is essential in the unit.

Outline a Sequence of Teaching Points

After all this preparation, it will finally be time to outline a sequence of teaching points. When I do this, I am usually not totally sure which teaching points will become minilessons and which will become mid-workshop teaching points or share sessions. Those decisions often come very late, as I revise my unit.

You will want to make your plans within general time constraints. For example, I might say to myself, I will use about three days for teaching kids to highlight the central ideas in their information writing. You'll approach a set of days, then, feeling sure about the most important skills that you want to teach, and the most important content you want to convey. Then you'll decide on strategies that will help students be able to do this work. For example, in this instance, I decided that to help students highlight the central ideas in their information writing, I should teach them to reread their writing, looking for the ideas they want to especially highlight, to stretch out the parts of their writing related to those ideas, to use introductory sentences and topic sentences to highlight those ideas, and to use text features in ways that accentuate the shared ideas. In this way, I had that progression of teaching in mind before beginning to write specific minilessons.

Before you can write a minilesson, you usually name a practical, how-to procedure that writers can use to achieve a goal. For example, if I want students to use text features to highlight what a text is really about, I need to do that work myself, watching the tiny steps I take to accomplish the goal so that I can articulate that sequence to students as they work together to use text features to highlight central ideas in our class text. You can't teach students this strategy in a minilesson or a mid-workshop teaching point or a share until you've figured out the content you want to teach.

Of course, whenever you teach anything worth teaching, you need to anticipate that students will encounter trouble. When I teach kids ways to highlight the central ideas in information writing, for example, I need to anticipate that this will pose difficulties for some kids. At least half your teaching does not involve laying out brand-new challenges but instead involves coaching and supporting kids to develop the skills they need to tackle predictable challenges.

When you plan a unit of study, you'll find that it is crucial to foresee the difficulties kids will encounter in the unit. You'll want to provide students with the scaffolding necessary to succeed with first a pared-down version of what you are teaching and, eventually, with higher-level work. For example, I knew I would need to provide some scaffolding for kids when I first taught them to write an essay that compared themes in two different pieces of literature. I knew that some students would find this confusing. To scaffold their work, I first demonstrated by planning my own compare/contrast essay aloud with them, showing them how I got ideas from the two texts and showing them how I made my writing plans. Then I asked students to try this on their own, with my process in mind.

Although you can predict lots of the difficulties that students will encounter as you teach them, it is inevitable that new and different issues will emerge. So you'll keep your ears attuned and your eyes alert. As you teach a unit, you'll outgrow yourself and your best teaching plans in leaps and bounds.

Write Minilessons

In writing workshops, students generate ideas for writing, and then they select one of those to develop. They make an overall plan—perhaps using a timeline, table of contents, or a boxes and bullets outline—then they revise that plan. They try a few alternate leads or introductions—and then get started. They write with some tentativeness, expecting to revise what they write with input from others.

The process of authoring a unit of study is the same. You'll generate an overall plan for the unit and revise it. Eventually you'll settle on a plan and get started. After all that planning and revising, you'll write the first word. Even then, you write knowing that your teaching plans will be what Gordon Wells refers to as "an improvable object" (*Action, Talk, and Text: Learning and Teaching Through Inquiry*, 2001).

If teaching plans are only in your mind or only coded into a few words in a tiny box of a lesson-plan book, then it's not easy to revise those plans. But ever since human beings inscribed the stories of hunts on stony cave walls, we have learned that once we record our thoughts and plans, the community can gather around those thoughts. Those thoughts can be questioned, altered, and expanded. The ideas of one person can be added to the thoughts of another. In scores of schools where I work closely with teachers, we keep a binder for each unit of study. In that binder, they keep a collection of all the minilessons that are related to a unit. Many of these are minilessons one teacher or another wrote, but others come from professional development that teachers have attended or books they've read. In these binders, the teachers also deposit other supporting material.

Hints for Writing Minilessons

- **The Start of the Connection:** Try to think of the first part of your connection as a time to convey the reason or the context for this minilesson. You are hoping to catch students' attention and to rally their engagement. Sometimes this is a time to step aside from writing for just a moment, telling a story or reliving a class event in a manner that will soon become a lead to (or metaphor for) whatever you will teach. Then, too, this is often a time to bring students together to recall and apply what they have already learned that functions as a foundation for this new instruction. If you have trouble writing the start of a minilesson, it is also possible to settle for simply saying, "Yesterday, I taught you . . ." and then referring to the exact words of that teaching point. These teaching points will generally be collected on a chart, so you can gesture toward the chart as you talk. Ideally you can follow this with a memorable detail of someone who used the strategy or applied the teaching point during the preceding day's minilesson. You can say something such as "Remember that . . . ?"

- **The Teaching Point:** The teaching point will only be a sentence or two in length, but nevertheless it merits care and revision; it is the most important part of your minilesson. Plan to repeat the exact words of your teaching point at least twice in the minilesson. To learn to create teaching points, try temporarily staying within the template of these words or something very close to them: "Today, I will teach you that when writers _____, they often find it helps to _____. They do this by _____." The important thing to

notice in this template is that you are not saying, "Today you will do this." A teaching point is not the assignment for the day! Instead, the teaching point is a strategy that writers often use to accomplish important writing goals. Then, too, notice that teaching points do not simply define the territory within which one will teach. That is, if a teaching point went like this, "Today I will teach you how to write good leads," then there would be nothing worth remembering in the teaching point!

- **The Teaching:** When planning how the teaching will go, begin by deciding what your method and materials will be. If you will be demonstrating using your own writing, go back and look at a few minilessons in which I used a similar method, and at first follow the template of these minilessons. You will probably see that I set students up to participate or to observe. Then I may tell the story of how I came to need the strategy, and act out what I did first and next. Alternatively, I may recruit students to join me in trying to use the strategy, and once they are participating, I do my work in ways that allow them to watch what I do and compare my work to what they were en route to doing.

  Either way, I often include in my demonstration an instance when I do something unhelpful, and then I correct myself, coming back on track. Throughout the demonstration, I tend to write no more than four sentences; usually these are added to an ongoing piece that threads its way through much of the unit.

  I might demonstrate using a bit of a published author's text instead of my own writing; again, if you decide to create a minilesson using that method, find instances when I did this and let them serve as an exemplar for you. You'll find that if I am demonstrating using a published author's text, I'll enact what the author probably did, prefacing my enactment with a phrase like "So and so probably did this. He probably . . ."

  I might choose not to demonstrate. Instead, for example, I might explain something and then show an example. These kinds of minilessons are more challenging to write, but again, I encourage you to find and follow a model as a way to induct yourself into this work.

- **The Active Engagement:** Almost always, the active engagement will be a time when students try the strategy that you have just taught, and they do so by writing-in-the-air (talking as if they are writing) to a partner. For example, if you have taught that toward the end of their work on a text, writers reread their own writing to ask, "Does this make sense?" then you'll want to use the active engagement time as a chance to provide students with some scaffolded practice doing this. You have two common options. One option is for you to say, "So, right now, while you sit in front of me, would you get out your own writing and read just the first paragraph as if you are a stranger, asking yourself, 'Does this make sense?' If you spot a place where it is confusing, put a question mark in the margin." The advantage of asking students to try the strategy this way is that you help them apply the minilesson to their own work and also help them get started at it. The disadvantage is that sometimes kids can't use the teaching point of the day on just any paragraph (as they could in this example), and therefore it is not possible for them to find a place in their current piece where the strategy applies and put the strategy into operation all within just a few short minutes. This portion of a minilesson shouldn't take more than four minutes! Then, too, you can't provide much scaffolding or do much teaching off this work because each student will be working with a different piece of writing.

You might, therefore, say, "Would you help me with my piece by becoming a reader of my next paragraph? Would Partner 1 read it quietly aloud and, as you read, think, 'Does this make sense?' Partner 2, you listen and give your partner a thumbs up if yes, you think it is making sense." By using your writing for the active engagement, you have a common text to discuss if problems arise in applying the strategy. Also, when students have applied the strategy to your writing, they can also transfer the strategy to their own writing once the minilesson is over and they are on their own. Otherwise, the teaching of the minilesson won't carry into the workshop time and may be less likely to carry into each student's writing life.

Sometimes the active engagement portion of the minilesson does not involve partner work; each writer works individually, often guided by the teacher's nudges. Teachers listen in on what students do, sometimes intervening to lift the level of a particular student's work. You will often end the time by reporting back on the good work one student did.

- **The Link:** During the link portion of the minilesson, you will usually repeat the teaching point verbatim, adding it to a chart as you do so. You won't have one amalgamated chart that lists every teaching point that has ever been taught! Each chart will feature a collection of strategies writers can use to accomplish a particular goal. That is, the title of the chart generally names the goal, and then below this there will be a growing list of strategies writers might draw upon to accomplish that goal. Charts lose their effectiveness if they are too long. Typically, charts do not contain more than five or six specific items.

Generally, the link is a time for you to tell students when to use what you have taught them. You will be apt to say something like, "When you are [in this situation as a writer] and you want to [achieve this goal], then you might use any one of these strategies," and you reread your charted list. "Another option would be to use this strategy," and you add the new strategy to the list. Usually, in the link, you will say something like, "So today, you have lots of choices. You can do this, or that, or this, or that."

Planning Conferences, Assessments, Homework, and the Rest

Planning a unit can't be equated to just writing minilessons! First of all, once you have planned a sequence of minilessons, you can read through them, imagining the challenges they will pose for your students. You'll be able to ascertain that for some minilessons, many students will need extra support, and those will be good places to plan small-group strategy lessons. You may decide that on some of those occasions, you will go from table to table, providing close-in demonstrations when needed of whatever it is you hope students will do first, circling back for demonstrations of whatever you hope they will do next. For these extra-challenging minilessons, you will probably want to plan follow-up minilessons, devising those after you study the particular ways your students are encountering difficulty.

Then, too, you'll want to plan how you will assess students' progress. You might think that the time to assess is at the end of a unit, but in fact, it is wise to mark several whole-class checkpoints within the unit. One way to do this is to plan to use the checklists and rubrics we have included within this series. You might use them on your own (or with colleagues) after school, sorting students' writing in piles according to where it mostly falls along the learning progressions we've provided. You will certainly recruit students to self-assess their progress—setting them up with their ongoing work and the checklists most appropriate to their development and kind of writing, asking them to see for themselves where they are strong and where they can aim to grow. At these checkpoints, you might look back at their work since the beginning of the unit to see what teaching has and has not taken hold. A few days into a narrative unit, you may want to ask whether they are writing about focused events, organizing their narratives chronologically, and storytelling rather than summarizing, for example. Early in an essay unit, you may ask whether the students are gathering entries that contain possible thesis statements. If not, you'll need to plan and devise new sessions accordingly, so you will leave some time and space for sessions you'll create as a result of these assessments.

You can plan for any other aspect of your teaching as well. For example, you could plan how partnerships might be tweaked so that they support the goals of the unit. You might think about particular language lessons that English language learners may need in a unit. You will also want to plan the at-home work you expect students to do during a unit. This will be especially important for any units that require research. Often the only way to keep the pace of the unit going is to assign research-based homework so that the main work students are doing in workshop is the writing itself!

Because your units of study will be written down, you and your colleagues can put them on the table and think together about these plans. "What's good here that we can add onto?" you can ask. "What's not so good that we can fix?" And that yearly improvement, of course, is the goal for all of your teaching—it's the goal for these units we've crafted as well as for those you'll invent on your own with your colleagues.

The Teachers College Reading and Writing Project

Support Large- and Small-Scale Improvement in Literacy Instruction

The TCRWP has been a premier provider of professional development for educators in the area of literacy instruction for nearly 30 years. Based at Teachers College, Columbia University, the TCRWP is also a research organization, developing ideas and methods that are foundational to literacy instruction around the globe. The 70 full-time teacher-educators at the TCRWP support principals, literacy coaches, reading specialists, and teachers.

Members of the Project's staff have published books that are foundational to language arts instruction across the world. Notable among these are: *Pathways to the Common Core: Accelerating Achievement* (Heinemann 2012), which has placed on *The New York Times* list of top ten best-selling educational books; *Units of Study for Teaching Reading*, grades 3–5 (Heinemann 2010); and the newest resource, *Units of Study in Opinion/Argument, Information, and Narrative Writing, Grades K–8* (Heinemann 2013–14).

The TCRWP's long-term partnerships with schools, districts, cities, and nations has led the organization to engage in many aspects of literacy reform. The Project has worked closely with schools to help them:

- ◆ Use formative assessments more productively
- ◆ Support more inclusive classrooms
- ◆ Take literacy reforms to scale
- ◆ Construct demanding curriculum to challenge strong readers and writers
- ◆ Become more standards-based
- ◆ Engage in more explicit instruction of grammar
- ◆ Leverage reading and writing instruction within content-area studies
- ◆ Support effective teaching by becoming professional learning communities

Teachers College Reading and Writing Project
525 W 120th Street, Box 77
New York, NY, 10027
www.readingandwritingproject.com

Implementation and Professional Development Options

The Units of Study books are a curriculum—and more. Calkins has embedded professional development into the curriculum, teaching teachers the "why" and "how" of effective writing instruction. Through regular coaching tips and detailed descriptions of teaching moves, essential aspects of writing instruction are underscored and explained at every turn. The professional development embedded in this series can be further enhanced through the following opportunities:

➤ At Your School or District

Implementation Support for Units of Study Led by a Member of the Units of Study Team or RWP Staff Developer

Through a one-day intensive session, teachers can get started unpacking the series' components, grasping the big picture of effective workshop teaching, and gaining an understanding of how to integrate assessment into the curriculum.

Multiple-Day Staff Development for K–2, 3–5, or 6–8 Educators

Invite a Reading and Writing Project staff developer to work in your school or district, helping a cohort of educators teach reading and/or writing well. Support includes new curriculum materials and new assessments.

Leadership Support

Topics include planning for large-scale implementation, establishing assessments across the school or district, learning from walk-throughs, designing in-house staff development, and instituting cross-grade alignment.

Multi-day Institute for 40–300 Educators

Host a "Homegrown Institute" for writing instruction, reading instruction, or content literacy. Tailored to your district's needs, the instruction and materials are specialized for K–2, 3–5, or 6–8 sections.

➤ At Teachers College   Multi-day Institutes at Teachers College

Teachers College offers 8 institutes per year. Each of these is led by world-renowned teacher-educators from the project, with great experts joining as well. Institutes include keynotes, small- and large-group sections, and sometimes work in exemplar schools. Educators from across the world vie for the opportunity to attend.

- **Summer Institutes on the Teaching of Writing** (June, August)
- **Summer Institutes on the Teaching of Reading** (July, August)
- **Literacy Coaching Institute on the Teaching of Reading** (October)
- **Literacy Coaching Institute on the Teaching of Writing** (January)
- **Content-Area Institute** (February)
- **Argumentation Institute** (December)

For registrations and applications, go to **readingandwritingproject.com/institutes.html**

➤ Across the Country

Each year, the Reading and Writing Project will be offering one-day seminars for teachers and administrators. These off-site seminars are held in selected locations across the US and focus on topical issues such as the Common Core State Standards. The seminars are delivered by TCRWP leaders and are open-enrollment events.

For dates, locations, and registrations, go to **readingandwritingproject.com/workshops-study-groups/tc-seminars.html**

➤ Online from TCRWP

Classroom Videos

More than 25 live-from-the-classroom videos let you eavesdrop on Lucy and her colleagues' instruction in writing workshop classrooms. You will see students engaged in the writing of argument/opinion, information, and narrative texts. These clips model the Common Core minilessons, conferences, and shares you will engage in as you teach these units of study. The videos are organized into a variety of albums: by grade-level range, by Common Core text type, and with a Teacher Effectiveness lens.

View these videos at **vimeo.com/tcrwp/albums**

Resources

The Project posts important and useful resources throughout the year, along with examples of writing that students at every grade level, K–8, did during last year's units of study.

Visit **readingandwritingproject.com/resources.html**

Twitter Chats and Book Talks

On Wednesdays from 7:30 – 8:30 PM EST join Lucy and her colleagues for live chat sessions on topics supporting literacy instruction. Follow them at @TCRWP or search #TCRWP.

Visit **readingandwritingproject.com** for full support